THE ISLAND SERIES

LUNDY

THE ISLAND SERIES

LUNDY

by A. and M. LANGHAM

*With a chapter on the archaeology of
Lundy by K. S. Gardner*

DAVID & CHARLES
NEWTON ABBOT

Set in 11 on 13 pt Baskerville
and printed in Great Britain
by Clarke Doble & Brendon Limited Plymouth
for David & Charles (Publishers) Limited
South Devon House Newton Abbot Devon

To Alex and Jenny
and all the young friends of Lundy

CONTENTS

ILLUSTRATIONS

ILLUSTRATIONS

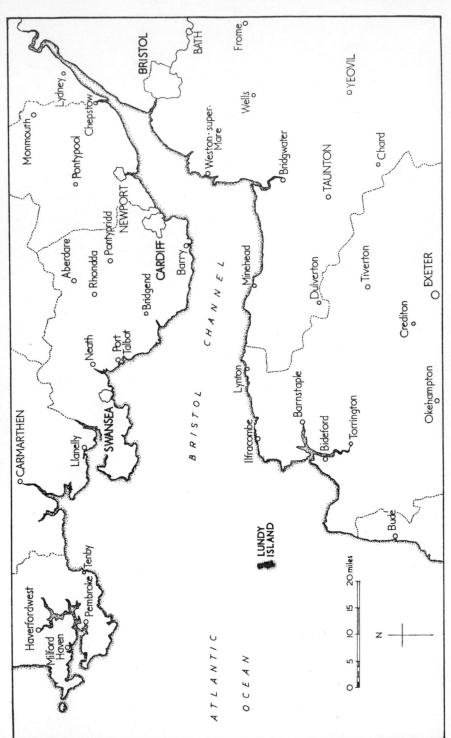

Lundy and Bristol Channel map

INTRODUCTION

W E have spent a holiday on Lundy at some time during each of the last twenty years and yet can still find each time some new facet to appreciate, as well as the pleasure of returning to familiar scenes and faces.

It is impossible to analyse the fascination which Lundy has for those of us who return there time and time again. We have tried to, and although we may say that it is isolated yet accessible, tranquil but not dull, remote but acceptably civilised, the right size to make a self-contained unit, beautiful and unspoilt— yet these do not add up to the whole, and we feel that no words of ours can do justice to the true qualities of the island itself.

In the early days of our discovery of Lundy we looked for books in which to find out more about it, but found that the two serious works on the subject were both out of print and difficult to find. We therefore began to collect whatever we could find about Lundy, and gradually became absorbed in a fascinating and seemingly endless study. The results of this study were collected into a book of which 250 copies were privately printed in 1959. Our researches continued and, as the original edition was quickly exhausted, we have now written this book in the hope that it will both interest those to whom the island is unknown and satisfy those who know it and love it as much as we do.

Reigate, 1969

MYRTLE LANGHAM
ANTHONY LANGHAM

1 PORTRAIT OF AN ISLAND

LUNDY, of all the islands around the coast of England, though quiet and remote, possesses a unique interest, springing from it character, its beauty and its varied history. It is a small, exposed island: a bold mass of granite some three miles long and roughly half a mile wide, lying almost north to south across the entrance to the Bristol Channel. The exact geographical location is: latitude 51° 10′ N, longtitude 4° 40′ W. The island lies nearer to the Devon than to the Welsh coast, and is linked with the mainland by the island boat which crosses the twenty-three miles from Bideford two or three times a week.

Here, within 1,100 acres, is a small self-contained world of utter tranquility, where there is no going anywhere except on foot. Walking about the island over the bouncy turf or beating back the invading brackens, the unhurried visitor can watch the soaring birds or the roaming animals; study the varied profusion of flowers, plants and insects; watch the rise and fall of the waves over the rocks; or climb about the rocky sidelands. Wherever he goes, the visitor will meet traces of the island's past. He may stand in the remains of a Stone Age hut; confront a medieval stronghold; wander the disused Victorian quarries; or pick up twisted pieces of a crashed German bomber. It is difficult to picture the scene a mere hundred years ago when 200 workmen were busy about the quarries, for nowadays the visitors can walk the island for hours without meeting anyone. Only a handful of people make their home here, either to work in the running of the island and the farm, or for the hotel and the summer visitors.

On this exposed plateau, date and time are of less importance than the moods of the wind and the sea. There is a tremendous exhilaration in walking, almost flying along in front of the galing wind and an overwhelming serenity in the quiet night, lit with the winking lights of the sea. There is a heavy uncertainty in the wandering mists swirling across the island, from the bare rock cliffs exposed to the Atlantic on the west to the bracken-covered slopes of the more gentle eastern side. This exposed position puts Lundy at the mercy of the elements, and the weather dominates the day-to-day life on the island, which can change from a restful sunny haven to a bleak wind-lashed rock. There is a piece of Devon weather lore :

> Lundy high, it will be dry,
> Lundy low, it will be snow,
> Lundy plain, it will be rain,
> Lundy in haze, fine for days.

The usual approach to the island is from the east, which reveals its gentlest aspect, for on this side the cliffs are softened by a green blanket of fern, and rhododendrons which, in the early summer, glow pink and mauve. On nearing the island, the silhouettes of the church and the tower of the old lighthouse break the line of the plateau, and the coastguard hut to the north becomes apparent. As the boat draws into the clear, vivid blue-green water of the bay and the noise of the boat engine dies away, the enfolding peace of the small anchorage descends and immediately the still atmosphere of the island is felt. The entire quarter-moon bay with its pebbly beach is dominated by the castle above, and the grey cliffs sweep down from the plateau past the shining white lighthouse to sink into the surf where Rat and Mouse Islands curve round in a protecting arc. Below the lighthouse are the remains of a concrete slip and jetty which were built in 1921 by the then-owner, Mr Christie, to berth the island boat *Lerina*. The lighthouse itself is reached by steps leading up from the landing beach, but as these are narrow and steep the heavy stores are landed by winch and cable which haul them directly from the ship. The lighthouse stands on a peninsula known as Lametor, which is joined to the island by a narrow saddle of crumbling shale separating the landing beach from Lametry beach on the other side, and sheltering the bay from the pre-

14

vailing westerly winds. At the south end of the beach, above high-water mark, are the crumbling remains of a fisherman's net store, and beyond the old, disused stairs to the lighthouse is Old Man's Cave, which can be reached quite easily, although it is obscured by the crumbling rock.

Visitors to Lundy disembark onto a wheeled wooden landing-stage, or by dinghy, and cross the shingle to the foot of the Beach Road to start the long climb up to the top of the island. Here stands a Trinity House marker stone which was the only survivor of the landslip in 1954, when an eighteenth-century limekiln, a hut dating from 1870, and an inscribed stone were destroyed. The stone, which had been placed there by Mr Heaven, made it clear that the island is private property and dates from an occasion when a dissident group of trippers disputed their rights with the owner. About a hundred years earlier another owner, Sir John Borlase Warren, started to build a jetty and had mounted on it a cannon brought down from an old battery somewhere on the east side. A widening of the path is all that remains of the jetty, while the cannon lies on the beach below. The capstan which stood here has been replaced by a motor winch, which is used to haul up the landing-stage and the small boats which are stored in the cave nearby. Beyond the cave, the path is protected by a buttress wall against falling shale. One such fall in recent years revealed a two-pounder cannon ball thought to have been fired from a ship and stated by the Tower Armouries to date between 1675 and 1724, at which time the island was the haunt of pirates.

Although it is called the Beach Road, the path is really a stony track just wide enough for the tractor to be used for haulage up and down. Before 1838, when this road was built, the difficulties of haulage must have been formidable, as can be imagined by looking up the old steep path which forks to the left beyond a ruinous cottage and sail loft. All supplies, even heavy furniture, had to be dragged up this old path by horses, and even with the new road horses were still used until the first tractor came in 1941. The road is bordered with ferns and wild flowers, and hereabouts grow the unique Lundy cabbages. On the seaward side, the cliff falls away sharply and the rocks are relieved only by a single pine tree standing in Lone Pine Gulch, where the road curves inland up to Millcombe Valley, and affords a most beautiful view of the East Side at Windy Corner.

No less beautiful is the path ahead through the valley, one of the very few places on Lundy shaded by trees. On the right of the path are the remains of the watermill which gave Millcombe Valley its name, and above it are three walled gardens. On the left at this point is a building, once a coal-store, in which a two-masted skiff, the *Heatherbell*, was built in 1887. Ahead is the disused carriage house and stable by the gate leading to Millcombe House, the owner's residence. When the foundations for the stables were dug in 1886, some human remains were found. A little waterfall runs into a drinking trough near the entrance to the stable, and from here the road winds zig-zag up until it joins the old steep path at the battlements.

This point is the junction of Lundy's three main 'roads': the old, steep path which bends sharply back and continues up to the castle; the road through Millcombe from the beach; and the road ahead to the plateau. The first is only a narrow footpath and has existed since early times; the second was built by Mr Heaven in 1838; and the third was widened to its present form in 1819 by Trinity House. Trinity House were of the opinion that it was impossible to construct a road from here to the beach, and so Mr Heaven proceeded to have this made at his own expense, acting as his own engineer. This junction used to be called Peeping Corner but the Battlements were later built there by Mr Heaven, as there was some danger that carriages and carts might go over the cliff when rounding the corner beyond a walking pace.[1]

Following the road inland, the traveller can fully appreciate the beauty of Millcombe House standing at the head of the green valley. It was built in late Georgian style in 1836 by Mr Heaven and is a delightful family house with a pleasant terrace in the front overlooking the gardens and the bay. When built, the house

Page 17: *(above)* Aerial view of the north end of Lundy taken from the south east; *(below)* the west side of Lundy

Page 18: *(above)* Aerial view of south end showing beach road, village and farm; *(left)* Devil's Slide, west side

was fitted with running water and washbasins—then a most modern innovation—but these were unfortunately removed during Mr Christie's ownership. The trees that surrounded the house were planted to give additional shelter, and many paths, now mostly overgrown, ran in various directions from the house.

On reaching the plateau, the road curves inland and crosses the common between the church and the main gate into the Manor Farm hotel.

The oldest part of the hotel was built in the early part of the eighteenth century, and was a small building with an archway in the middle, which gave access to a small courtyard that still exists. About 1840, Mr Heaven made alterations to it, removing the two small towers from the upper storey and filling in the archway. About 1864, the quarry company built what is now the tavern and old bakehouse, the outbuildings and the dairy, and began the southern wing which now contains the hotel lounge and dining-room. The wing was completed in 1896 and the building was then used as an hotel for the first time. The original part of the building, the Old Manor House, was used by the quarry officials, and later by the tenant farmers as a farmhouse. The building took on its present form in 1927 when the billiard room, with bedrooms above, was added, so joining the old building to the tavern. A generator supplies electricity to the hotel, and running water comes from a large reservoir built in 1900, the covered roof of which can be seen to the west.

The social hub of the island lies in the north wing of the hotel where the residents, visitors and lighthouse-keepers mix without distinction in the Marisco tavern and the general stores. The stores carry a comprehensive stock and have served as the post-office since the GPO left the island. The tavern was originally only a canteen, but now, as a public-house, is unique in the British Isles since it is not subject to licensing laws and is open when required. The whitewashed walls of the little bar are hung with lifebelts and lanterns salvaged from Lundy wrecks, and with photographs of both Lundy and Grassholm.[2]

The wall which encloses the hotel garden to the east was built

B

in 1871 and is pierced by an arched 'monastery gate' leading to the site of the corrugated iron church on the left, which was used from 1884 until 1897. To the right, a path across the head of the valley leads to a little corrugated-iron bungalow which used to be a schoolroom. The path ahead soon forks: on the right down to Millcombe House; and on the left to a rocky outcrop mysteriously called Hangman's Hill, where there is a small shelter known as the 'Ugly'. This is a sheltered vantage point at which to sit and watch the boats in the bay, with the hills of the north Devon coast visible across the Channel.

Passing behind the hotel, the main path now becomes known as the High Street, with the farm buildings along it on either side. Outside the tavern there is a small greensward with walled kitchen gardens to the west and the old piggery, which has now been transformed into a tea-garden to replace the building behind the hotel which fell into disrepair during the last war. To the north of the tea-garden is the Smithy, and then the Linney where the tractors and agricultural machinery are stored. Part of this building is now used as a shop on those days when there are large numbers of day visitors, and is commonly referred to as 'the supermarket'. Opposite this is the engineer's workshop which used to house the rocket signalling apparatus.

The old threshing house lies a little to the north of the rocket-shed, and is the oldest of the farm buildings. It was converted from a barn by the addition of the adjacent roundhouse, where a horse or donkey was harnessed to a gin to provide motive power for the machinery in the threshing room. The stables behind have been converted into pens for goats as it was intended that these should provide a supply of fresh milk, but this idea has been abandoned.

On the west side of High Street, beyond the Linney and the small field known as Pig's Paradise, are the shippens, built in a square round a central yard and now in ruins. The rick-yard and fowl-run are the next two enclosures and these face a row of cottages, originally built in 1870, which were rebuilt and modernised in 1966 to provide staff quarters.

High Street ends at a gate just beyond an enclosure called Bull's Paradise, and the gate itself forms the eastern end of the lighthouse wall. The path continues northwards alongside a large meadow which, in 1934, was marked out with whitewashed boulders as an airfield. A part of the wall alongside the path was removed to lengthen the approach run, and the windsock was fixed to an old telegraph pole near the centre of the field. During the Second World War trenches were dug across the field to prevent enemy aircraft from landing. The airfield is bounded on the east by the walls enclosing the Tillage Field and the Brick Field, from which a watercourse drains over the edge of the plateau in a small waterfall near Sugarloaf Rock. In days gone by, ships would anchor close inshore to replenish their supply of fresh water from this source. There was once a settlement in the Tillage Field known as Newtown, and although the last traces of this were cleared about 1850, the name persisted in use until quite recent times.

Quarter Wall, one of four which traverse the island, was begun by the notorious Benson, using his convict labourers, and was completed by Sir John Borlase Warren. The area to the south of the wall was known as South Farm, and that to the north as Middle Farm. Where the path crosses the wall, the Field Society have built a bird trap, and north of this are the foundations of twelve cottages built by the quarry company to house their employees. These houses stood derelict for some years then three were dismantled and used in the construction of the signal station in 1884 and stones from the remainder were used in the building of St Helena's church in 1896. The officers of the quarry company were housed on the eastern edge of the plateau in a block of three houses most beautifully sited to command a glorious view of the bay. The southernmost of these three houses was occupied until 1916. One other building associated with the company is the quarry hospital, a little further to the north, and there are some overgrown foundations of other buildings lying between the bird trap and the three Quarter Wall cottages.

By a pond a few yards north of Quarter Wall a small track turns east from the main path and leads down a marshy valley past some stunted trees and another pond to the first of the quarries. The track is joined here by a path which leads from Millcombe along the east sidings, and continues past the mouths of the quarries cut back into the hillside. The first quarry is tree-shaded and marshy and the path runs past it to a ruinous building that was a time-check office. The circular opening in the wall once contained the clock. From here the path descends steeply to the level of the main quarries, where a large ledge was constructed to provide a marshalling area for the cut stone. Now it is the site of another large bird trap built by the Field Society. The stone was lowered down to the quarry beach by a small tramway, now disappeared, but by using the narrow winding footpath from the ledge it is still possible to reach the beach below, where the outline of the old jetty can be traced.

The walk through the quarries is delightful and here and there the bracken gives way to honeysuckle, all manner of wild flowers and a few trees. One of the most pleasant spots in VC Quarry, named in 1949 when a memorial was dedicated there to John Pennington Harman on the fifth anniversary of his posthumous award of the Victoria Cross. John Harman was the eldest son of Martin Coles Harman and this had been his favourite playground as a child; the quarry now remains a most fitting place for this simple and proud memorial to a life sacrificed with great heroism.

From VC Quarry, the path continues northwards past the last of the quarries, in which the small drillholes made in the rocks to split them apart can still be seen. Rising, the path curves inland until it reaches the plateau again and meets the main path from which a diversion was made at Quarter Wall. The main path is marked by granite boulders, which were placed there after the coastguard cottages had been built, to provide a guideline to the lookout on Tibbett's Hill. Each boulder weighs two and a half tons, and it was not until they were all in position—and two of the horses used to drag them up from the quarries had collapsed and died—that it was discovered that the stones should have been one cubic foot in size, not one cubic yard!

To the west of this path the land slopes gently to a central pond, called Pondsbury, which is a favourite watering place for the cattle and wildlife of the island. Just before the path reaches the gate in Halfway Wall, there are the remains of a burnt-out German bomber which made a forced landing after an air raid on Swansea in March 1941. The crew escaped unhurt, set fire to the plane and were then taken prisoner and held at the hotel until they could be removed to the mainland.

Halfway Wall was also built by Benson's convicts but is shorter and in better condition than Quarter Wall, and it has on its north face a sheep-pen, which indicates that North Farm has carried sheep for some considerable time. At the far eastern end of the wall is a Logan Stone, but it can no longer be rocked. From Halfway Wall the ground rises gradually to Tibbett's Hill. Just to the south of this, over the eastern edge of the plateau, there is a rock formation which strongly resembles a helmeted human profile and this has been called the Knight Templar Rock. On the summit of Tibbett's Hill is the small robust building erected by the Admiralty in 1909 as a lookout, and from the observation room on the roof fourteen lighthouses can be seen at night. The building now makes a very pleasant small house which is let to visitors.

The northbound path passes to the west of Tibbett's Hill, the second highest point on the island, and then slopes gently down to Threequarter Wall, passing close to the remains of a circular building which is referred to as the Roundtower. The purpose of this building is as yet unknown, but it is possible that it was the base of the windmill mentioned in an account of a visit to the island made in 1787.[3]

Threequarter Wall, which divides North Farm in two, was built in 1878 by the tenant farmer, Mr Thomas Wright. Beyond the wall, the ground sloping gently down towards Gannet's Combe is the site of a medieval farmstead of the Long House type, in an original enclosure of some twenty acres. The origin of

23

its present name, the Widow's Tenement, is not known. Although this part of the island is now bracken-covered and deserted except by the wild animals, it was inhabited since early times as is shown by the remains of several hut circles in the vicinity.

The site of a coastal battery, dating from the Civil War, remains at the bottom of the eastern sidings nearby, just above high-water mark. Its name, Brazen Ward, suggests that brass guns were mounted here, though what has become of them is uncertain.[4] Traces of a small building still remain and the gun platform, which protected the natural landing-place below, commands a view south as far as Tibbett's Point and north to Gannet's Rock. Looking northwards from Brazen Ward, a curious natural rock formation, known as the Mousehole and Trap, can be seen very clearly; standing on a small projecting headland, it looks like an old-fashioned trap of a brick propped up on a stick near a hole in the rock. Between this and Brazen Ward is a curious cave called Queen Mab's Grotto, which was formed by the action of the sea before the land levels changed. The little beach below the cave is called, mysteriously, Frenchman's Landing.

Gannet's Combe, the lowest point of the plateau, is a wide, shallow valley, formed by the junction of three smaller valleys, which leads through marshes to Gannet's Bay, or Cove. These take their name from the large Gannet's Rock offshore, which was so called as far back as 1274 when its colony of gannets was valued at five shillings a year, a large sum in those days. The deep vegetation of the valley is in sharp contrast to the denuded rock which forms the north end of Lundy. The peaty soil there was completely destroyed by accidental fires in 1933 and 1935, and only now is simple vegetation once again slowly re-covering the rock. However, this misfortune had its compensations in that it revealed an extensive ancient settlement of late Neolithic, or early Bronze Age, covering the whole of the island north of Gannet's Combe.

At the very north end of the plateau there is a small ruined building called John O'Groats House, though no one knows why.

It appears to have been in use as a watch house during the Civil War, as there are traces of at least two fortifications near sea level close by. In the summer of 1960 a rectangular room was uncovered at the base of Puffin Slope, some hundred yards west of the north-east fortifications, and this seems also to date from the Civil War. It had a large fireplace, still showing traces of ash, and a granite seat to the right of the hearth. A further part of this defensive complex was found in 1966 when a small room was discovered about 15 ft below the plateau, some 40 yd north east of John O'Groat's House.

The East and West Side paths converge a few yards short of the end of the plateau at the steps down to Lundy North lighthouse on the north-west point. At the foot of the steps there is a tramway, which is used to carry stores to the lighthouse from the top of the nearby cable hoist. Watching the tide-race roaring among the rocks, it is difficult to imagine that underneath North-West Point there is a tunnel 300 ft long and 30 ft high where a freshwater spring, the Virgin's Spring, bubbles up through the salt seawater. This spring is almost certainly merely drainage from the plateau through faults in the rock.

A path runs beside the tramway and leads to steps which have been cut in the rock down to sea level. From these steps a remarkably close view of the nesting seabirds in Kittiwake Gully can be obtained, and also the best view of Constable Rock, which legends say was a Cornish giant who came to Lundy to rid it of snakes and other reptiles. Having done so, he was turned into this 30-ft high column of granite—a rather shabby reward.

Below and beyond the lighthouse is a small, abandoned lookout which was built for the Admiralty coastguards at the same time as Tibbett's. North-West Point used to be a breeding site for gannets but after the construction of the lighthouse the birds gradually abandoned it and there are no records of nests there after 1903.

After the long climb up the steps from the lighthouse, the anticlockwise tour of the island can be continued along West Side path. The West Side of Lundy is in sharp contrast to the East

Side, and as the path here follows the plateau edge more closely, the striking beauty of the stark rocks lapped by the clear foaming water can be enjoyed for much of the way. From North End to the Old Light the west path runs for the most part alongside the telegraph poles that carry the line linking North Light with the buildings at the south of the island.

The west path skirts a bay, the coast of which is called Long Roost,[5] and runs parallel with the east path as far as the site of the Widow's Tenement, passing a smooth granite slope running from the plateau edge down to the sea, aptly known as the Devil's Slide.[6] Near here is a double-decker cave, the remains of two adits made during a search for deposits of copper ore. The path continues round the coast of St James's Bay, past St James's Stone at the southern end, and on towards Threequarter Wall. A little to the north of the wall lies a large circular piece of granite, 54 in in diameter, with a central hole and smooth on one side; although this is always called the 'millstone', no satisfactory explanation for it has yet been found. After the stile in Threequarter Wall has been crossed, another human-shaped rock form comes into view, this one known as Ally Sloper, or Gladstone Rock, from the prominent nose. The path passes the sources of three small springs, one of which has been dammed to provide a drinking place for the animals, and then skirts the picturesque Jenny's Cove, where the *Jenny*, carrying a cargo of gold dust and ivory, was wrecked in 1797.

At the point where Halfway Wall reaches the cliff edge a platform has been constructed, where, in medieval times, a stone-throwing machine, or mangonel, is thought to have been mounted. This would have defended the landing-place below, near Pyramid Rock, which is a point of access still used occasionally when easterly winds make a landing in the bay impossible. Halfway Wall itself extends well over the western sidings, though the remains of a horizontal wall near sea level and the traces of a wall some 150 ft below the platform are probably associated with earlier fortifications. It has been said that one of the tenant farmers stored a boat here which he carried down to the water's edge on his back, possibly in an attempt to salvage some of the *Jenny's* valuable cargo.

The granite pinnacles south of Halfway Wall are curiously stacked and rounded and have been aptly named The Cheeses. Just over the edge, a little further to the south, is a spring known as the Butler's Pantry, by virtue of the fact that it never goes dry! The Devil's Chimney, a tall column of rock at sea level, is another of the 'diabolical' features of this side of Lundy. The west path is now crossed by a small stream flowing from Pondsbury into Punchbowl Valley. This steep and grassy little valley, with the stream falling in a series of miniature waterfalls, takes its name from the large granite bowl, 4 ft in diameter, which lies by the stream some little distance down. The bowl existed when Grose wrote his description of the island in 1775 and he conjectured that it may have been a font. It could have been the lower half of a millstone, but it is impossible now to be sure either of its original purpose or site. The bowl was broken during the last war and subsequently repaired by members of the Field Society.

Between Punchbowl Valley and Quarter Wall, the granite is split by a series of chasms some 10 to 20 ft wide and varying in depth from 20 to 80 ft. Local tradition holds that they, together with Earthquake Rock which lies just south of Jenny's Cove, first appeared after the famous Lisbon earthquake of 1755. The effects of this earthquake were felt elsewhere in England, and it is not impossible that this may indeed be the explanation of the faults. There are the remains of a second German bomber a little way down the cliff south of the Earthquake but on this occasion, April 1941, the plane failed to find the plateau and crashed into the cliffside, all the crew being killed. As Quarter Wall is approached from the north, the path runs close by the cliff edge above a quarry where worked blocks of granite and the remains of iron handrails can still be seen. This quarry was possibly the source of building stone for the construction of the Battery which lies at the bottom of a steeply descending path to the south of the wall.

The Battery is one of the most pleasant places on Lundy. It

was built in 1863 to supplement the Old Lighthouse, and in foggy weather, fired a round of blank shot from two eighteen-pounder guns every ten minutes, as it had been found that during fog the lighthouse was usually obscured. After 1878, guncotton rockets were used instead of the guns, and when the new lighthouses were built in 1897 the Battery was abandoned. There are two ruinous cottages, one of which once housed a family of thirteen, and these are separated from the gunhouse by a small flight of steps hewn from the granite alongside three small outbuildings. Two guns were kept inside the gunhouse. The one in use was placed centrally on the grooved floor, which is sloped to reduce recoil, and had its muzzle projecting through the front window. The building was roofed with corrugated iron, so that in the event of an explosion the roof would blow off and reduce blast. The gunhouse is now empty, with the cannon, bearing the cipher 'GR', mounted on either side.

On rejoining the west path and continuing southwards, the Old Light soon stands out on the skyline across Ackland's Moor. This area, named after a previous tenant farmer, is bounded by the remains of a wall to the west which Mr Heaven built in 1872 in an attempt to protect the field from rabbits. The moor now forms the western end of the airfield and was the site of the short-lived Lundy golf course.

The Old Light stands at the highest point of the island, on Beacon Hill, and until 1968 was the headquarters of the Lundy Field Society. During the season, members of the society would stay there and assist the resident warden in observing and recording the wild life of the island. One of the outbuildings was converted for use as a laboratory as a memorial to Mr M. C. Harman, who as owner, founded the society in 1947. From the top of the lighthouse tower on a clear day the range of view extends from Skokholm in the north-west to Bude in the south-west, and embraces all the Bristol Channel to the east. From here can be seen the Cornish Tors, Brown Willy and Rough Tor and the Cornish coast to Trevose; St Govan's Head and the Prescelly mountains of Pembrokeshire; and from Exmoor Tors beyond

Bideford Bay to the grand sweep of Carmarthen Bay and the Gower Peninsula. The lantern platform also affords a fine view of the island in its entirety and, in particular, a clear impression of the ancient chapel in the cemetery near the base of the tower.

At present we know little more about this chapel than that it was a small, solidly constructed, rectangular building said to have been dedicated to St Elen with 'the oratory dedicated to St Anne'. A visitor, writing in 1787, states clearly that the entrance was from the north and adds that it was 'length about 25 ft, breadth 12 ft, doorway 4 ft, thickness of wall nearly $2\frac{1}{2}$ ft.'[7] Within the bounds of the chapel are five graves of members of the Heaven family, and it was while the most northerly of these was being dug in 1905 that the Tigernus stone was discovered. Apart from the four ancient inscribed stones, of which the Tigernus stone is one, there are many unmarked mounds as well as the headstone graves which date from the last century and the boulders which mark the graves of Mr M. C. Harman, his wife, and their second son, Albion.

To the east of the cemetery there is a small stone cottage within a walled enclosure, which was probably built at the same time as the Old Light for the use of the Corporation agent, a Mr Grant, who was collector of customs at Barnstaple. Before the days of steamships, adverse weather often forced the collectors to remain on the island for some time until sailing conditions improved. This cottage is now called Stoneycroft.

From the Old Light, the land slopes gently to the south and forms one large field, called West Side Field. The site of a small enclosure known as the Friar's Garden has been lost, but it is thought to have been near the Parson's Well—which gives rise to some interesting conjectures. Various herbs, such as woad, have been found growing in the garden. A third relic of the Second World War can be found a short way down the cliff near here, where a British 'Whitley' bomber crashed during thick fog in June 1942 with the loss of all its crew. At the water's edge near here is Pilot's Quay, so named after the Bristol pilots who used it for landing during easterly winds, to await the arrival of ships requiring their services. The quay and footpath were badly damaged during gales and earthslips in 1910 and 1911, since when they have been largely disused.

At the extreme south-west point of the island is a large pyramidal rock, of which the landward face is sheer. It is known as Great Shutter Rock, local lore holding that it would, if reversed, fit exactly the funnel-shaped cavity of the nearby Devil's Lime-kiln. This awesome rock, softened by the gentle colourings of lichens, was the site chosen by Kingsley for the wreck of the Spanish galleon in his novel *Westward Ho!*, and just a little to the north was the scene of the actual wreck of HMS *Montagu* in 1906.

The Devil's Limekiln is a huge natural funnel in the rock near the cliff edge; it is 250 ft wide at the top and its sides slope almost vertically down to converge 300 ft below at sea level, where a narrow passage admits the foaming sea. Further east, along the south coast, in Seal's Hole, which runs inwards for 2-300 ft from an entrance about 50 ft high and 20 ft wide. The cave ends in a chamber estimated to be 100 ft high and is named after the seals which are believed to breed there. Above it, on the plateau, there is a pretty, small pond where golden carp can be seen swimming in the clear water and wild flowers overhang the banks. The pool takes its name from the nearby rocket pole, which was erected by the Board of Trade in 1893 for testing the rocket lifesaving apparatus.

The footpath continues eastwards along the southern end of the plateau and very soon passes the Kistvaen (see Chapter 3), accidentally discovered in 1851. The coast here, and to the east, forms a large bay known now as The Rattles, or Rattles Anchorage, but once known as Rattles Landing Place.[8] The junction of granite with the shale (see Chapter 3) runs from a point in the centre of this bay towards the north-east. In 1853 a small quantity of copper was found and, although soon abandoned, the horizontal workings made by the Cornish miners can still be entered. They lie below Benjamin's Chair, a flat grassy ledge hidden a few yards below the cliff. It is said that this name originates from a ship of that name which was wrecked in the bay below. The sole survivor of the disaster managed to climb up to the ledge, only to die of exhaustion.

The path lies eastwards through a gate and passes close to Golden Well before joining the crossroads at the head of St John's Valley, where the paths from the beach, the castle and the south coast meet the path to the hotel.

2   GEOLOGY, CLIMATE AND LAND USE

ALTHOUGH Lundy is of considerable interest to geologists, the only comprehensive study of the geology of the island is that made by Dr A. T. J. Dollar entitled 'The Lundy Complex, Petrology and Tectonics', which was published in *The Quarterly Journal of the Geological Society* in September 1941. Dr Dollar writes that 'Lundy is a granite mass, the denuded core of far more lofty mountains piled up during the Amorican folding. When these upheavals in the earth's crust occur, half-liquid magma pushes up into the cavities at the base of the mountainous folds of rock and solidifies; then, as millions of years go by with their millions of seasons of rain and frost, first the lofty peaks are denuded away, then the lower and larger masses, until a time may be reached when the granite core, the solidified magma so much harder than the overlying rocks, is all that remains.'

University research undertaken in 1962, using modern techniques, concluded that the Lundy granite was fifty-two million years old, plus or minus an error of two million years. The southeast corner of the island alone is now composed of the remains of the overlying slates that once covered most of the island, and which have been remorselessly worn away by the action of centuries of varying climates and abrasive winds. The junction of this slate with the granite forms a distinct line from the Sugar Loaf to the Rattles, and is so similar to the Morte slates of North Devon that it can be called Upper Devonian.

There are several intrusive dykes of igneous rocks, one of which forms a vertical face that can be seen from the landing beach, and which prevents further erosion of the shale on which the castle stands. This particular form of microgranite is unique and has been named Lundyite.

32

In the nineteenth century, Mr Heaven employed some Cornish miners to drive an adit at the junction of the slate and granite just east of Benjamin's Chair, where copper ore had been found, but the amounts found were so small that the venture proved uneconomic. Adits were also driven to explore a copper vein near Long Roost, but again the quantities were trivial. Later, a company was formed to exploit the granite and a description of its activities will be found in Chapter 8. During the Second World War there was a shortage of molybdenum, but although an inspector visited the island at the suggestion of Mr Harman, the small amount present on Lundy was not considered worth exploiting. A list of the other minerals present on Lundy will be found in Appendix G.

That part of the north of the island was covered by ice during the last Ice Age is the opinion of Professor G. F. Mitchell, who made a study of pebbles found in this area in 1965/6. He concluded that the foreign pebbles present had been deposited by the ice and that Gannet's Combe may have been formed by meltwater draining to the east.

Climatic conditions on the island are profoundly affected by the prevailing westerly winds, and Lundy's position in the middle of a tidal channel. The west winds rush with unbroken force over the plateau, and have even been known to blow livestock over the cliff edge, quite apart from denuding the surface vegetation. Fortunately, gales of such severity are rare, but the wind does have a permanent influence on the vegetation, and thus all but one of the trees on Lundy are found on the sheltered east side.

The climate is generally more equable than that found on the mainland, a fact noted by Mr Heaven, who kept a record of the temperatures over a number of years. He found that the mean was seven to twelve degrees higher on Lundy in the winter, and a corresponding drop of about the same amount was experienced in the summer. He attributed this to the modifying influence of the Gulf Stream, a contention borne out by the comparative rarity of snow and ice on the island. Lundy does, however, experience a considerable amount of mist and fog, and the signal guns

33

at the Battery, which were used as a fog warning, are known to have been once fired continuously for seventy-two hours.[1] An unusual feature of the fog is that it frequently covers the plateau only, leaving the beaches and sidelands clear.

The rainfall mean tends to be slightly less than that of the mainland, probably due to the upward deflection of the westerly winds. There have been times when both North Devon and South Wales have been affected by rain and storms while Lundy has remained clear. A certain amount of salt-water spray is thrown up on the West Side, and during strong winds the delightfully-named Lundy Butterflies, clusters of sea froth, are found on the plateau grass. Except during a prolonged dry spell the rainfall is adequate for the island's needs, but the water available for domestic use depends on conservation. The hotel is supplied from a covered reservoir in the south-east corner of the lighthouse field and several storage tanks have been built recently to supply the dwellings on the south-east corner of the island.

The more northerly part of the plateau is similar to the West Country moors—undulating scenery, with green, brown, grey colours predominating, especially to the north. The eastern sidings are sheltered, thickly overgrown with bracken and uniformly steep. Three valleys break this pattern, Gannet's Combe in the north, and St John's and Millcombe in the south, which all give access to the water's edge. The soil depths vary from nil near the north end to almost six feet in some deep gullies but the average depth is about one foot of humus and acid soil overlying silt. In hollows this readily forms marshes, and towards the north end it closely resembles peat. The north has been denuded of soil by fires on at least three occasions, the present extreme poverty being due to an extensive fire in the 1930s, caused by careless visitors.

South Farm, that area south of Quarter Wall, is divided by Lighthouse Wall into two parts. The southernmost of these contains the village and farm and the main cultivated portion of the island. North of Lighthouse Wall is permanent pasture, except for patches of bracken and for the Tillage and Brick Fields to the east, which are enclosed for the cultivation of cereals as cattle

Page 35: *(above)* Millcombe Valley 1897. The walled gardens are cultivated but no trees are visible; *(below)* owner's residence, Millcombe

Page 36: (above) Cottages inside the castle keep; (below) the castle from the south west

feed. Middle and North Farms are not cultivated, although they provide rough grazing in some parts. That cultivation was at one time more intense than is the case today is clear from the existence of these names and from the presence of traces of enclosing walls which still remain in these areas.

The earliest description of Lundy cultivation is to be found in the Inquisition, or Survey, made in 1274, when a jury reported :

> That there may be there twenty acres of arable land which may be sown with barley or oats; each acre is worth per annum two pence, whether tilled or not. There are also five acres of meadow, worth three pence an acre, also pasture for eight oxen and twenty cows with their offspring for two years. Also, that in all, the pastures can bear sixty-eight head of cattle also four mares and one stallion, with their offspring for two years, to wit, thirteen head. There is also there pasture for three hundred wethers and two hundred ewes with their offspring for two years, to wit, pasture for nine hundred sheep. Also the taking of rabbits is estimated at two thousand, and the estimate is at five shillings and sixpence each hundred skins because the flesh is not sold; also, the rock of Gannets is worth five shillings; also other birds but they are not sold. There is also an eyre of butcher falcons, which have sometimes three young ones, sometimes four. This eyre the jury knew not how to estimate, as they build their nest in a place in which they cannot be taken . . . in summer, even in times of peace, it is necessary to have fourteen servants and a Constable to watch the defences of the island, and in winter, ten servants.

The jury valued the island at £7 6s 2d. On the back of the Inquisition is the note :

> The jurors, being asked by him who made the extent, what the turf, gorse, brushwood, and the fresh water were worth to the King's benefit, answered that none of them could take value, as no man would buy them; but the auditing clerk perceives that all these things may be considered of such value to the keepers of the island as to lessen their wages to the extent of five shillings, and the fowls besides; although they cannot be sold, nor are the keepers willing to eat them, yet he estimated them at forty pence. Of quarries, minerals or timber, none was found there. As for the flesh of the rabbits, what it is worth to the keepers of the island he leaves to the discretion of the King's Counsel to estimate.

c

Be it mentioned however that for all these matters the keepers of the island have been wont to take nothing less in wages.

From the foregoing it is very evident that the civil service mentality is nothing new—one wonders if the keepers were able to hold out for their full wages.

An inquisition held in 1321 gives a further picture of Lundy in the middle ages, after it had been forfeited to the Crown by Sir John de Wyllenton. He had 'held the island with all its appurtenances, in which is a certain castle with a barton (farmyard) for which they made no valuation, as the same was destroyed and burnt by the Scots'. The depredations of the Scots also destroyed much of the rabbit and bird life which had been a source of revenue to the islanders. At this time there were

eight tenants, who hold their land and tenements by a certain charter of Herbert de Mareis granted them for the term of their lives, who pay fifteen shillings yearly. Also one tenant, who should keep the said gannets during the whole of the season of their breeding, and for which services he will be quit of his rent of two shillings. . . . There are in demesne forty acres of arable land worth yearly ten shillings; also, two hundred acres of pasture land worth 16s 8d per annum; also three acres of meadow worth 2s 6d; also waste land by estimation 200 acres worth yearly 8s 4d, so little because all the tenants in the island have common on it.

Sir Thomas de la More[2] stated that Lundy 'aboundeth with pasture ground, and oates very pleasant. It bringeth forth conies very plentiful, pidgeons and other fowles. It aboundeth altogether with victuals and is very full of wines, oile, hony, corn, braggot (mead), salt, fish, flesh, and sea or earth coales.' This last sentence has been quoted in an attempt to prove that England 'formerly produced wine from grapes' but the original passage differs from the translation given above, and merely shows that these goods were present on the island, not necessarily native produce.

At the end of the sixteenth century Lundy suffered from the piracy that was rife in the Bristol Channel and was neglected by its owners, the Grenville family. Westcote, writing about 1620, describes the poor state of affairs there: 'that it hath been tilled . . . the furrows testify yet plainly . . . neither will any man try again; there is so little hope of profit. The most profit that is now made of it is by hogs, conies and sea fowl.' No trees were left on the island except 'stinking elders', in which starlings were present in such numbers that it was impossible to approach the trees for their droppings. This barren picture is confirmed by Risdon, writing in about 1630, who mentioned the rabbits and Lundy livestock, but stated that the chief commodity was still sea fowl, which he described as being so abundant that it was necessary to exercise care to avoid stepping on the eggs. Camden completes this picture by telling us that 'there are about 500 acres of good land but the best part, for want of cultivation, is covered with furze and heath and the whole land swarms with rabbits and black rats . . . thickets at the south end'.

The island recovered from this period of neglect and an account of it is given by John Sharp, who had lived there for fifty years and who probably left about 1700. The old man remembered a population of about 100 people who were engaged in tending cattle, and in the sale of feathers, skins and eggs as well as growing 'exceedingly fine barley, potatoes and almost every kind of garden stuff in great abundance'. It is believed that about 1720 the island was being farmed by a Mr Scores.

In 1752, the stock on the island was given as twenty cows, two bulls, thirty bullocks, seven sheep, seven horses, thirty hogs, sixteen deer, and seven goats, although a note adds that the flesh of the pigs was uneatable, being yellow and strong. Benson, as tenant, set fire to the overgrown vegetation but did little to improve the farm and he it was who introduced the deer, some of which still remained there in 1777. Sir John Borlase Warren attempted to re-establish the soil by planting trees and on two paintings of the island which he commissioned in 1775, and which now hang in the Cardiff Exchange, trees are clearly shown.

In 1776 a professor of Botany at Cambridge, the Rev Thomas Martyn, visited Lundy and reported:[3]

that about 500 acres thereof, situate at the South End, were covered with a coarse grass and might feed lean Welsh cattle;

but all the rest of the island was, in his judgment, incorrigably barren, and bore little else to cover the rock but heath and moss; and that were there was any soil the staple was mostly very shallow and incapable, without very great expense, of any considerable improvement; and that the island was so high, and so subject to winds, that it would be difficult to grow corn to much advantage; and that it was so over-run with rats and rabbits that any crops that might be produced thereof would, as he apprehended, be infallibly devoured by them; and he was persuaded no trees had ever grown upon the said island, nor could be forced to grow thereon to any purpose, without great care, expense and difficulty; and that the said John Borlase Warren having caused many trees to be planted on the said island in the spring of the year 1775, the deponant found that the same were all withered and dead; and that in his judgement the greatest advantage that could be made of the said island would be by agisting of cattle, but there would be great drawbacks upon that advantage from the great expense which would necessarily attend upon the carrying of cattle to and from the nearest land, which is about three leagues; and that the said island is distant eight leagues from Ilfracombe, which is the most certain port and place where proper vessels could be procured to carry passengers, cattle, or goods; and that there was but one dwelling-house and the remains of an old castle on the said island, the said dwelling-house being small, and in a very ruinous state and condition; and that he, the said Thomas Martyn, was better able to depose with respect to the soil of the said island, as he had made Natural History and Agriculture the chief study of his life.

More interesting than this rather despondent report is the record of a visit of inspection made in July 1787 by Mr Cleveland, the then owner, and a party of friends. The island was at that time divided between tenant farmers and . . .

the morning of Saturday, the 7th July, was appropriated by our traveller and Mr Cleveland to arranging disputes among the tenants, and swearing in Mr Hole Constable of the Island. . . . The north part is now incapable of being improved . . . nothing vegetable grows on it. . . . About the middle of the island the land is low. . . . In this lowland are a few willows, about as high as brushwood. . . . Of the rabbits, the inhabitants take about

1,000 couple yearly, principally valued for their skins : their flesh is consumed on the island except a chance Ilfracombe boat comes by, to purchase a few . . .; about 160 acres were then inclosed, in fields of 7, 8 and 10 acres each; the produce wheat, barley, and oats. . . . The inhabitants sowed but small crops, trusting to their birds and rabbits to pay their rent. (£70 per annum).

The writer then goes on to describe the exploitation of the birds, as follows :

we walked to view the rocks on the western part of the island, and saw vast quantities of wild fowl and the method of taking them in nets. . . . Every morning and evening the natives watch their nets and take out the birds that are entangled. They catch in a good season 1,700 or 1,800 dozen, and make 1 shilling per pound of their feathers. People from the neighbouring coast are hired to pluck them, at twopence per dozen, and pluck about four dozen per day. . . . The natives collect these (birds) eggs, and send to the Bristol sugar refineries. The Muirrs are the most profitable, twelve of them producing one pound of feathers. After being plucked they are skinned; these skins are boiled in a furnace for the oil they yield, which is used instead of candles; and the flesh is given to the hogs, who feed on it voraciously.

The visitor then describes the netting of birds on Gannet's Rock :

the method of conveying them, when taken, to the island, is by means of a rope, fastened at each end to the island and rock, on which hangs a basket to a pulley, which is drawn occasionally backwards and forwards with the birds. The people run great hazards in taking them out of their nets, and sometimes lose their lives.

In 1788, indeed, Mr Hole, the island constable mentioned above, lost his life in this way.

A tenant farmer at this time was a Mr Budd, who left in 1791. By 1794 there were eighty head of cattle, 400 sheep, twelve deer, and pigs and poultry. Some 400 acres were under cultivation, 300 of which were arable lands, and the rest pasture. Wheat was the main crop at this time, which marks a significant improvement in the island's land use. During the Napoleonic Wars, the whole of Middle Park was sown with grain, and it is thought that this made it the largest single field ever used solely for this purpose in the British Isles. The pasture land was extended to about 5–600 acres, of which 300 acres were enclosed, and milk from the island's cows was noted for its remarkable richness. Sea birds continued to be an important part of island life, and Loyd records that 379 lb of feathers were plucked in 1816. The season started on 1 August each year, and on one day as many as 700 puffins were sent to Clovelly at the opening of the season, followed by 500 the next. During the fortnight the season lasted, it was calculated that 9,000 birds were destroyed, and this annual slaughter was not stopped until Mr Heaven bought the island in 1834.

The new owner made great efforts further to improve the stock and to raise the standard of farming, and although these improvements suffered a set-back when the farm was leased to the granite company, who neglected it, by 1875 280 acres were enclosed, drained and cultivated. Eighty acres were devoted to barley, oats, potatoes, mangolds, turnips, rye and flax, the rest being used as permanent pasture. There were 600 sheep, and seventy head of cattle, and a considerable stock of pigs, turkeys, geese, ducks and fowls. About this time, the fishing was let at £10 a year, and each season brought catches of over 2,000 prime fish for export, including lobsters, crabs and crawfish. Daily catches of as many as 1,000 herrings were sometimes reported. To obtain these catches, the seal population had to be held in check, and a seal gun found in the Marisco tavern in 1911 was probably used at this time by the fishermen. An attempt was also made to form an oyster bed, but when it was first swept in 1853 it proved disappointing.[4]

In 1850, the tenant farmer was Mr John Lee. He left the island in 1861 and was succeeded by Mr Blackmore, of Bishops Lydeard, who stayed for the next fourteen years. The Rev H. G. Heaven continued his father's practice of leasing the island farm to tenants and in 1885 the whole island, with the exception of the owner's house and grounds, was let. By then, the stock had risen to 900 sheep, 100 head of cattle, including thirty milch cows, fifty horses (with an additional three mares for riding and carriage use, six draught horses and a stallion), and pigs and poultry. The tenant farmer, Wright, built Threequarter Wall and brought all the land on the west side of the main track, together with that south of Quarter Wall, under cultivation. Beyond Threequarter Wall, and between Quarter and Halfway Walls, the land was left wild.

Wright gave up in 1891, and Henry Ackland then took over. A visitor in 1894 wrote: 'Wheat is now very rarely grown, as it does not pay. Oats is the principal crop, and in 1890 it was very abundant. . . . Rabbits were sold at 6d each. £100. [was realised in the sale of rabbits] The man came over, caught the rabbits, paid 6d per head.'

The Rev H. G. Heaven planted many trees in Millcombe and St John's valleys, which are now mature and have completely transformed the valleys.

By 1925, when Mr Harman became the owner of Lundy, stock had fallen to about 600 sheep and eighty cattle, plus pigs and poultry, and although grouse, partridge and pheasants were introduced, only the pheasants survived. An attempt in 1929 to inhibit erosion and provide shelter by planting 2,000 Japanese larch trees was a failure, probably because of the rabbits and deer, and there are none on the island today.

The stock figures for 1931 show that there were several hundred sheep, twelve cows, one bull, a few Devon heifers, twenty goats, thirty deer, some ponies, one donkey, seventy-nine Chinese geese, and innumerable rabbits. This remained roughly the state of the island agriculture until 1939 and the outbreak of the Second World War, when the Devon war agricultural committee visited Lundy, and estimated that some 500 acres could be ploughed for potatoes and oats. The island's 20-year-old and only horse was considered inadequate for this job and a 2-ton Fordson tractor was brought across in a naval vessel. Members of the Women's Land Army were sent across to assist with the ploughing and planting.

Post-war developments on the island have seen the rise of sheep again, and there are now about 350. They are sold ashore regularly, most being sent by sea in the island boat, though naval landing craft and even aeroplanes have been used from time to time. In 1955, the semi-wild animals were estimated at 100 deer, forty-five goats, eighty-five Soay sheep and a considerable herd of wild horses. Efforts were made to reduce these numbers in 1956 and 1957, after which there remained about thirty deer, twelve Soay sheep and twenty-seven goats.

Regulations designed to eradicate bovine tuberculosis led to the last of the Red Devon cattle being shipped to the mainland early in 1958. Later that year, an attested herd of twelve Galloway cows and a bull was imported, and these now form the nucleus of the island herd. As they are beef cattle, an attempt was made to supply Lundy with fresh milk from pedigree goats, but this was not a success, and all milk is now imported in powder form.

Rabbits on Lundy were first mentioned in the thirteenth century and this is believed to be the earliest reference to them in England. They were not affected by the myxomatosis epidemic during the 1950s but, nevertheless, their numbers appear to have declined and the most recent estimate is about 4,000. The rabbits are not exploited commercially, but provide occasional sport for visitors.

Several attempts were made by Mr M. C. Harman to introduce new varieties of animal to Lundy. He established a distinct breed of Lundy pony by a cross between New Forest ponies and a Welsh Mountain stallion, but although a company was planned to develop the breed, none was ever registered. At various times squirrels, wallabies, peafowl, swans and many deer were introduced, but with the removal of the peafowl in 1955 only the deer remain. Both brown and black rats are a great menace to bird life on Lundy, but there are no mice, moles, hedgehogs, snakes or other reptiles.

Thus, although it will always be necessary to combat the effects of wind and soil impoverishment, the island has at least managed to disprove Professor Martyn's despondent dicta of 1776; and there is still scope for more intensive farming.

3 HISTORY OF LUNDY-1

THE historical vicissitudes through which Lundy has passed stem mainly, of course, from its situation just off the coast of Devon. An ideal jumping-off place for invasion of the coast, it was also a place of refuge if things went wrong, and a well-nigh impregnable natural fortress. Small wonder, then, that for centuries the greatest importance has been attached to possession of the island, and that the Crown has always been interested in keeping a tight hold of, or at least a close watch on, the occupiers. Vikings, robber-barons, pirates, Royalists, invaders, Scots, and refugees from justice, have all found Lundy a tempting refuge or a base for their operations. Space allows only a brief sketch of the island's history and though it can hardly hope to do justice to the many dramas played out on Lundy, it should at least afford some idea of the fascinating background to the island.

Archaeological finds have shown that Lundy was inhabited in prehistoric times. So far, three main sites of prehistoric settlement have been found; one in the south-east corner of the island, another to the north of Threequarter Wall, and the third north of Gannet's Combe. The first site was investigated by Dr A. J. T. Dollar in 1932, and finds of worked flints, side scrapers, end scrapers, a small hollow scraper, a knife, a hand chopper or bone crusher, and several pot boilers were found. About 500 flint flakes were collected in the Brick Field, and others were found in the Tillage field and St Helen's. The pot boilers indicate the use of fire and simple pottery but, so far, no pottery of comparable antiquity has been found. It is thought that there should have been in the same area some remains of hut circles, which have probably been destroyed during ploughing, and that several large upright stones still standing may well be the remains of menhirs.

The second site is clearly marked on the Ordnance Survey map, but on the ground the evidence is not easy to trace, and it is possible that the walls were robbed to contribute to the building of Threequarter Wall. When the remains were investigated in 1954,[1] some fragments of flint and chert were classified as undoubted artifacts, showing signs of a worked cutting edge, the other fragments being knappers' waste. A small handsaw was also found, together with two pieces of sandstone which are thought to have been whetstones. A little to the west of the hut circles is an opened tumulus.

The third area covers the whole of the plateau north of Gannet's Combe and was exposed by accident, following the fire of 1934. It consists of a series of walled enclosures, with at least eight circular huts within them; three of the huts have a very distinct ground plan. The remains show that they had a very well-marked doorway to the south-east, which is delineated by large, upright granite blocks. Considerable amounts of flint waste have been found over the site, especially to the immediate south-west of John O'Groats House, and various worked flints, including two scrapers, a knife, and a double-ended core, were discovered. A large quantity of limpet shells have also been unearthed here, which may be direct evidence as to the dietary habits of primitive inhabitants.

Two other sites of interest, a tumulus on Tibbetts Hill, and the Kistvaen on the south-west of the island, are thought to be contemporary to, and connected with, the settlements described. The tumulus was excavated by Loyd in 1922, who found :

a roughly squared granite block . . . which, on being raised, disclosed two similar blocks, parallel to each other and at right angles to the first. Among the earth thrown out, two small pieces of flint were found.

The Kistvaen was much larger, and as he describes it :

. . . consisted of a horizontal elongate granite slap or cap-stone about 1 ft 6 in thick resting upon upright stones of the same material that enclose between them a space of 6 ft deep and about the same in width, and contained a small fragment of pottery.

The three settlement sites are considered to date from the Neolithic or early Bronze Ages—that is, some 3,000 years ago—although the double-ended cores found usually date from the Mesolithic period. The precise dating of artefacts found on Lundy must always be something of a problem, for it is recognised that isolated island communities did not progress at the same speed as those on the mainland. The Lundy settlers would have been further hampered by the lack of raw materials suitable for primitive economy, notably the lack of flint and chert. All the flint used must have been carried up from the beaches, where it would have been washed up by the sea.

A survey of the old field boundaries in June 1963, north and south of Halfway Wall, revealed the plan of an old farmstead, complete with small, rectangular field plots and two associated buildings. One of these buildings, a flat circular platform on a natural rise in the ground some 100 yd north of Halfway Wall and 50 yd west of the eastern track, was trenched, and proved to be a circular hut 30 ft in diameter. The occupation level yielded flints and early Iron Age 'A'-type pottery. Other plots and huts are thought to exist to the north-east of this settlement.

Evidence that Lundy was inhabited in the Dark Ages comes from four datable indications; inscribed stones, pottery, beads and burial forms. So far, four inscribed stones have been discovered in the Beacon Hill cemetery and these apparently date from the fifth to the ninth centuries AD. The first stone was found fortuitously when a grave for a member of the Heaven family was being prepared within the chapel grounds in 1905, but the inscription was not noticed until 1923.

Similar to several found on Cornish stones, the inscription has been translated: 'In memory of Tigernus, son of Tigernus', and the style suggests that it commemorated a Romanised Briton. Three more stones were subsequently discovered, all dating from the period of Roman influence, as well as some Dark Age pottery and beads, all indicating that a flourishing and artistic community existed on Lundy during these times. (See Appendix A : The Archaeology of Lundy).

47

After the eighth century, Viking raids on the British coastline became increasingly frequent, and gradually the raiders came to make bases of the various islands around the coasts or in the mouths of rivers. Raids were made up the Bristol Channel in 795, directed against South Wales, and in the ninth century the North Somerset coast and the Taw estuary were attacked. In 878 the Viking chieftain, Hubba, left South Wales and crossed the Bristol Channel for a foray in North Devon. He was defeated and killed near Appledore, and there remains an unsupported theory that the 'Giants' Graves' are those of Hubba and his men. There are many other records of Viking raids in the Bristol Channel, and Lundy must have been familiar to them, both from its position in the mouth of the Channel, and from its strategical value as a temporary base. Lundy is mentioned in the famous Orkneyinga Saga as the refuge of a piratical Welsh freeman, who, realising the island's fortress potential, managed to defy any raiding or punitive expeditions sent after him. The Welsh influence is thought to be marked in the early history of Lundy; for the original chapel was dedicated to a Welsh saint, St Elen and, indeed, the first mention of the island in the Pipe Rolls gives its name as Ely, a shortened version of Eliensis, meaning of St Elen.

The Normans came to North Devon in 1068, and in the summer of that year the eldest son of King Harold led a force of sixty-four ships from Ireland to the mouth of the Taw, where they were defeated by the Normans.[2] The date of the arrival of the Normans on Lundy is not known, but the early records show that the de Newmarch family held the island about 1140–50. The first mention of the Marisco family, in connection with Lundy, occurs in 1154, and in 1166 they held the island from Henry de Newmarch for the fifth part of a Knight's fee.

In 1163 the North Welsh kingdom sent a messenger to Lundy to seek help in their struggles against Henry II. This messenger may have been Prince Madoc himself, but in any case the de Mariscos were at this time loyal to the English king and it is

48

MARISCO FAMILY TREE

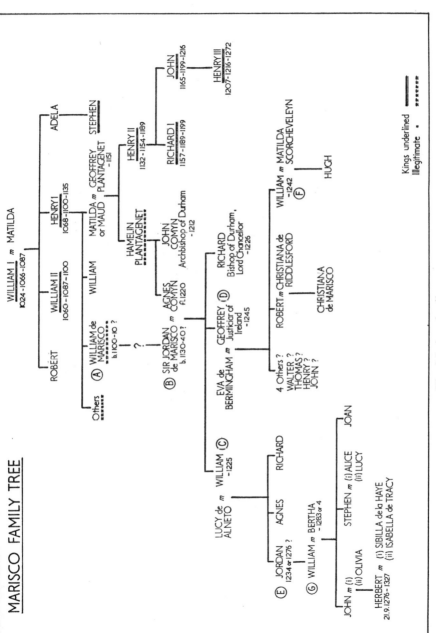

The Marisco family tree

Kings underlined ▬▬▬
Illegitimate • ▬ ▬ ▬

unlikely that they would have risked his wrath by assisting the Welsh. A few years later Madoc fled from Wales and led his followers in an expedition westwards, when it is thought that they made their departure from Lundy.[3]

Originally a great Norman family, the de Mariscos had spread throughout Europe to such an extent that Henri IV of France referred to them as the first house and family of Europe after the Bourbons. The English branch of the family may be descended from a Geoffrey de Marisco who came over with the Conqueror in 1066. Alternatively, it is now known that one of Henry I's many illegitimate children was known as William de Marisco. Possible inferences to be drawn from this fact are discussed later.

The de Mariscos were known to be on Lundy during the reign of Stephen, but in 1155 Henry II commanded the return of all the royal lands granted away in Stephen's reign. Either the Marisco's tenure of the island was of longer standing or they chose to flout the order, for they remained in possession. In 1160, Henry tried to grant the island to the Templars, but again the island was not surrendered and fines were levied in lieu; William de Marisco is recorded as owing a fine of 300 marks in 1194 and again in 1195 for retaining custody of the island against the wishes of the King and the rights of the Templars.

Following his accession to the throne in 1199, John confirmed the grant of Lundy to the Templars, and also stipulated that they should pay rent for some lands in Somerset as long as 'William de Marisco shall holde the island of Lunde against the King's will and theirs'. However, the de Mariscos maintained their hold, which caused the unfortunate Templars to plead for possession. A record of 1202 states that the Templars still owed rent for their holding of Marisco lands in Somerset, while William de Marisco still owed 120 of the 300 marks he had been fined. In the same year, the Sheriff of Devon was given forty marks for the defence of the ports against William; it seems that William was using Lundy as a pirate base for raids on the North Devon coast. William seems to have steered his course through the turbulent

50

politics of John's reign with some skill, for when the King quarrelled with the Church, he seems to have made his peace with authority and been appointed to the charge of some of the royal galleys, as well as being given a further grant of land. The Templars were forced to relinquish their claim to Lundy for 100 shillings.

In 1216 William sided with the Scots and French against the King and was captured by the English while serving with the French fleet off the Kent coast. In 1217, Henry III came to the throne, and an amnesty was declared. William was restored to Lundy in return for promises of loyalty and good behaviour. He was also later allowed to move stone-throwing machines—mangonels—to Lundy. He died peacefully in 1225, and was succeeded on Lundy by his son, Jordan, who seems to have been less warlike than his father.

William's brother, Geoffrey, was Justiciar of Ireland at the time of William's death, and had a son who was also called William. The Marshal of the King's lands in Ireland, Earl Richard, was on very friendly terms with Geoffrey de Marisco, but when Richard rose in revolt against Henry III, Geoffrey remained loyal to the Crown. However, on the defeat of the rising, both Geoffrey and his son came under suspicion of complicity in the revolt and were fined 3,000 marks, while some of their relatives were fined and imprisoned. They were not released from prison until late in 1234, long after other associates of the Marshal had been freed, and the King confiscated three of their castles as pledges for their future fidelity.

Geoffrey and William travelled to London in an attempt to vindicate themselves, but came up against an enemy, Henry Clement, who had been sent to Court by the new Justiciar of Ireland. William accused Clement of influencing the King against him, while Clement openly boasted of his part in suppressing the rebellion. At midnight on Sunday, 13 May 1235, sixteen men appeard outside Clement's lodgings. Six of the party entered and, finding Clement at home, murdered him. Suspicion naturally fell on William de Marisco, who fled at once westwards, making for Lundy. His father, Geoffrey, took sanctuary at Clerk-enwell, and some of their adherents rushed off to East Anglia until the hue and cry died down.

William, with his wife and household, duly reached Lundy, whereupon the rightful owner, William the son of Jordan,[4] made haste to disassociate himself from his cousin, and to clear himself with the King, who, evidently convinced that William alone was responsible for Clement's death, had allowed Geoffrey to leave sanctuary unmolested.

Once safely on Lundy, William turned to piracy and to a policy of harassing the royal authority in any way that offered. In 1237, William seems to have made an alliance with King Alexander II of Scotland, who was on the point of war with England. Henry was obliged to prepare ships to attack Lundy and to safeguard his own ships crossing from Ireland, which had been attacked by the vengeful William. The seige was not pressed, however, until an attempt on Henry's life was made by an agent of the Mariscos. The King, holding court at Woodstock, was confronted by an intruder who, pretending to be insane, called on Henry to resign his kingdom to him, saying that he bore the sign of royalty on his shoulder. The King was unperturbed by these ravings but when, that night, armed with a knife, the man broke into the royal bedroom—the King, fortunately being elsewhere—the alarm was raised and the agent overpowered. He confessed to the plot, implicating William de Marisco, and was torn limb from limb at Coventry.

Efforts to bring William to book were now intensified. Direct methods having failed, it was resolved to capture the rebels by stealth. In May 1242, William Bardolf, a Norfolk baron, with thirteen armed men managed to land on Lundy and capture de Marisco. 'William was betrayed by one of his men whom he had detained on Lundy against his will. The rocks protecting the place could only be scaled at one point and William imprudently set this man to guard the weak point. It was a misty day and William was sitting at meat when the King's man came.' It was probably the mist that rendered the attack possible, as under

52

Page 53: *(above)* A party of bellringers at St Helena's Church, Rev H. G. Heaven in centre of back row; *(below)* St Helena's Church under construction, 1896

Page 54: *(above)* The hotel, High Street and farm from the church tower before 1939; *(below)* Marisco Tavern

MARISCO TAVERN & GENERAL STORES

such conditions the harbour is not visible from the plateau, and Bardolf could land unobserved.

The captives were taken to Bristol, and subsequently on to London, where William and five others were lodged in the Tower, the rest of his band being imprisoned in the Fleet and Newgate gaols. William and his adherents were tried and convicted of high treason and murder, and were sentenced to death by royal warrant.

> The said William, after sentence had been passed on him, and when on the eve of suffering death, so long as he yet lived, constantly affirmed, invoking the judgement of God, that he was free from and utterly guiltless of the crime of high treason charged against him and the same of the death of the before mentioned clerk (Henry Clement) and that his only motive for withdrawing to the island had been by avoiding to turn aside the anger of the King, which by whatever judicial expiation, or other humiliation, it had always been his first wish to appease; but when he had fled to the Island, and called some friends to his assistance, he was driven, as he said, to support his wretched existence on necessities snatched from every quarter. Pouring out his soul then before God in confession, he acknowledged his sin to J. de St Giles, one of the order of preaching friars, not betrayed into expressions of malice in his own excuse but rather accusing himself. And thus with soothing words of consolation the discreet preacher and confessor dismissed him in peace, persuading him to sustain his approaching death as evidence of penitence.

He died on 25 June 1242,

> . . . being first dragged from Westminster to the Tower and thence to the . . . Gibbet, when he had there breathed out his wretched soul, he was suspended on a hook, and when stiff in death was lowered, disembowelled, his bowels burnt on the spot, and his wretched body divided into quarters which were sent to the four principal cities in the Kingdom, by what pitiable spectacle to strike terror in all beholders.[5]

There are so many contradictions and problems in the history of the de Marisco family and their association with Lundy that some events are difficult to understand. It is known that the first member of the family to incur the royal displeasure was Jordan, for some unrecorded misdemeanour, and yet despite this and the fact that the de Mariscos had held Lundy against the wishes of the King and in the teeth of attempts by the Knights Templar to take just possession of it, they were later granted the manor of Braunton. Again, although William de Marisco had been captured amongst the French in 1217 he was soon released and allowed to return to Lundy, and even to fortify it. Remembering the words

William de Marisco on his way to execution

of the would-be assassin of Henry III, they may even have been claimants to the throne of England. If the family were descended from a royal bastard,[6] they may well have considered their claim to the throne stronger than that of any of the rulers after Henry I, as all the descendants who reigned were from the original Norman line on the distaff side. And this might well have accounted for the consideration they received and the powerful emotions they aroused.

Once the de Marisco occupation had been brought to an end, the Crown promptly took steps to secure control of the island and make sure that it would never again harbour disaffected elements. The importance which Henry attached to Lundy must have been considerable, judging both from the many references to it in the Rolls, and from the fact that one of the most powerful men at Court, William de Cantilupe, who was Seneschal of the royal household, was sent to report on the measures taken on the island to secure the king's power. During 1242, fortifications were put into repair on the king's orders, and although the onset of winter delayed the construction of a castle, it was eventually completed in May 1244. The population of Lundy at this time was in the region of fifty persons, comprising the garrison under the constable, and some farmworkers who farmed the lands for the king.

Following a series of royal governors, in 1254 the king made a gift of Lundy to his eldest son, Edward, 'to be held of him and his heirs for ever'. Edward was then only fifteen, and the island was left in the charge of the keeper, William la Zuche. During the barons' revolt, the island was put under the protection of the barons of the council, where it remained until Prince Edward defeated de Montfort and was able to resume control of the kingdom.

By 1281, the de Marisco family were again in evidence, but though they managed to persuade the king to recognise their right to the island, their claim continued to be disputed elsewhere. In 1321, the disputant was Sir John de Wyllington, who was in rebellion, and to ensure the safe keeping of the island the king took it back into his own possession.

Lundy reflected the struggles for power during the troubled reign of Edward II, being first granted to the favourite Hugh le Despencer, and then sacked by the Scots in 1321. When Roger Mortimer finally defeated the king, forcing him to fly to Chepstow in 1326, Edward and the Despencers had planned to seek refuge on Lundy and actually put to sea to try and land there, but contrary winds forced them back and the royal party was taken at Neath Abbey, the Despencers killed, and the king imprisoned, deposed, and eventually put to death in Berkeley Castle.

The de Mariscos still kept their interest in Lundy throughout these vicissitudes, but luck, or royal favour, was not with them, and the island passed finally to William Montacute, Earl of Salisbury. Salisbury determined to end all doubts as to the possession of Lundy, and managed to agree with all the claimants, including Stephen de Marisco,[7] that for a monetary consideration, their claims should be waived. The island remained in the Salisbury family until 1390.

For the next 300 years Lundy was passed from one family to another, at all times being reckoned a valuable holding. In 1462, the island was granted to the Duke of Clarence, but passed to the Crown when Clarence was drowned in his butt of Malmsey in 1478. In 1534, it appears that the island was uninhabited, for an appeal for help was made by the crew of a Spanish caravel, who had been put ashore on Lundy 'to perish of hunger' after their ship had been seized by pirates while trading along the coast. There are other records of piracy at this time; a gang of French pirates, under their captain, Devalle, seized Lundy and preyed upon the Bristol traders. Clovelly fishermen mounted an expedition against them, which succeeded in burning the pirate ships and capturing the whole gang.

During the reign of Elizabeth, an interesting point arose concerning Lundy. Bishop Turnstall was making a peace treaty with the Scots, and reported:

> The Isle of Lundy being excluded from the treaty on the part of England, and the Lordship of Lorne on that of Scotland, he requests further instructions, these being without precedent. The men who best know her chronicles should be consulted herein, lest unawares she gives away part of her Crown.[8]

To which the Queen replied:

> as regards the suggested omission of the Isle of Lundy and the Lordship of Lorne, she will not alter the ancient order of treaties.[9]

During Elizabeth's reign, the family owning Lundy, the St Legers, lost a considerable sum of money and were obliged to part with some of their possessions. The family applied to the Grenvilles, who agreed to make them a loan in return for the fee-simple of Lundy. The families were later united when the heiress of the St Legers married Sir Richard Grenville. When Sir Richard set off on his voyage to the New World, Sir Walter Raleigh was named as one of the trustees ordered to administer his estates, including Lundy, for Mary Grenville.

Piracy in the Bristol Channel was then on the increase, following the rise in the volume of shipping passing through it. Three of the better-known pirates who definitely used Lundy as a base were Robert Hickes of Saltash, who was there between 1576 and 1578; Captain John Piers of Padstow, who was there in the 1560s and 1570s; and John Challice, sometime between 1574 and 1581. The Barnstaple authorities launched an attack on the island in 1587, and succeeded, at a cost of 5s 5d, in capturing 'divers rovers and pirates'.

Still, however, the pirates continued to use the island, and in 1595 the Queen herself addressed a rebuke to Sir Barnard Grenville for his neglect of his inheritance, and threatened to take Lundy into her own hands. The pilotage notes for the Spanish Armada recorded that Lundy would make a good refuge, and the state papers noted that Lundy was likely to be used by malcontents plotting against the regime. In 1608 matters came to a head and complaints were made at Barnstaple, but little was done until 1610, when the Lord Lieutenant of Devon and the Mayor and Corporation of Barnstaple were empowered to send a force against the pirates. Any goods or ships seized were to be retained by them in return for the expenses incurred in the expedition. This led to a protracted wrangle as to the division of the hoped-for spoils, which delayed matters for a further two years. At last the expedition sailed and chased the pirates off to Milford Haven, capturing four prisoners. A pirate named Salkeld had planned to have himself crowned as Pirate King of Lundy, but a revolt among his men caused him to flee the island. Whether the neglect was the cause or result of pirates inhabiting the island we do not know, but it was thought secure enough for Grenville to offer it to a kinsman, Sir Lewis Stukely, as a refuge from the odium caused by his arrest of Sir Walter Raleigh on orders from King James. A social outcast, Stukely died insane on Lundy in 1620.

In 1625, it was reported that three Turkish pirates had occupied Lundy, capturing its occupants, and were threatening to burn Ilfracombe. A government inquiry was ordered, for this attack had aroused widespread alarm out of all proportion to the damage caused. The 1630s appear to have been the heyday of the island's use as a pirate lair. The notorious Captain John Nutt made it one of his headquarters, styling himself Admiral, and leaving his 'Vice-Admiral', one John Smith, in charge there. Sometimes, though, the island was the target for raids, as in 1633, when a Spanish man-of-war landed eighty men to sack and plunder it. An account of this raid says 'they burned our farms, took away our young sheep and our daughters and left us only old ewes and old women'—the sheep it will be noted, took precedence of the women! Following this outrage, the government commissioned Captain Sir John Pennington, himself a former pirate and now in command of HMS *Vanguard*, to end the pirate menace once and for all. He was given absolute powers, but even so, two pirates were reported at Lundy the following year, and Algerine rovers were using the island as a base in 1635.

The depredations and excesses of the Turkish raiders did much to bring home to the English the horror of piracy and no doubt helped to bring about its ultimate suppression; but by 1640 the conflict between King and Parliament began to overshadow all else.

HISTORY OF LUNDY-2

THE Civil War greatly affected Lundy, and the island's natural advantages as a fortress were exploited to the full for the benefit of the Royalist party. Sir Bevil Grenville, who had succeeded in the inheritance of the island, devoted himself loyally to the King and on his death in 1643 Charles appointed Thomas Bushell governor of Lundy, granting him the custom duties on lead, and leases of the royal mines in Wales and in Combe Martin. Bushell had learned the principles of mining, and had opened a mint at Aberystwyth Castle, from which he supplied the King with coin and precious metals during the struggle.

The growing Parliamentary threat to Wales led Bushell to increase his interest in the silver-lead mines of Combe Martin in Royalist Devon. Lundy provided a natural stepping-stone between Wales and Devon, and there is also evidence that Bushell was fond of the island for its own sake. He re-fortified the castle,[1] using guns recovered from a shipwreck in Bude Bay, and built several coastal fortifications, of which the Brazen Ward is the best remaining example.

With the decline of the Royalist cause, Bushell retired to his fortress, continuing to hold out for the king, and remained on Lundy with his garrison long after the mainland had capitulated to the Parliamentary faction. His continued presence there was an embarrassment to the new government, but they found themselves unable or unwilling to try to overcome him by force. Lord Saye and Sele had negotiated with Parliament for the purchase of Lundy, but the man in possession was naturally unwilling to let him enter into occupation. A stalemate ensued, and in January 1645–6 the government decided to treat with Bushell. The governor of Swansea Castle was authorised to write to Bushell and offer him terms, suggesting that if he surrendered at once he might be able to make a bargain with Parliament for the repossesion of his mines. Nothing came of this, as Bushell argued that he had been given the island by royal authority, and only the termination of his trust by the same source would be sufficient quittance of his duty. Some months later, Lord Fairfax asked him to come himself, or to send a deputy, to negotiate a surrender. Bushell, unwilling to abandon his position of strength, followed the latter course and, perhaps to ease his conscience, wrote to the captive king asking permission to surrender his trust :

> May it please your Majesty,—The enclosed I have received from my Lord Say's servant, who is Governor of Swanzey, which I conceive was sent by his Lordship's direction, wherein he invites me to the surrender of this isle, being his Lordship's known purchase; in perusal of which I was not at all startled at the threats therein, but must confess myself moved by the obligations it minds me of, with which I formally acquainted your Majesty in the presence of my Lord of Dorset, since which Captain Crowther, Vice-Admiral of these seas, summoned me to surrender this place. And not long after Sir Thomas Fairfax sent a drummer with his letter and an order from the Committee of Both Kingdoms, wherein they proposed their assistance in restoring me to my interest in the silver mines if that I would deliver up this island to my Lord Say. Your Majesty well knoweth how I have maintained Lundy at no other contribution but my own, and how cheerfully I have exposed my friends and my own credit for your service, as well as exhausted them in the discovery of the mines royall; besides the place in itself is useless except in some advantage it may yield to me. If your sacred Majesty would be pleased to vouchsafe me leave to express my gratitude to my Lord Say by my quiet and free surrendering it, which I hope your goodness will not deny me, but if otherwise your Majesty shall require my longer stay here, be confident, Sir, I shall sacrifice both life and fortune before the loyalty of
>
> Your obedient, humble servant,
Thomas Bushell.
Lundy, 14th May, 1646

This letter resulted in the following, rather touching letter from the King :

> Bushell,—We have perused your Letter, in which We finde thy care to Answer thy trust We at first replaced in thee. Now, since

the place is unconsiderable in itself, and yet may be of great advantage to you, in respect of your mines, We do give you leave to use your discreation in it, with this Caution, that you do not take example from Our selves, and not be over-credulous of vain promises which hath made Us great only in our sufferings, and will not discharge your debts.[2]

With the royal assent given, Bushell was able to set about negotiations for surrender with a clear conscience, determined to drive a hard bargain with Parliament. He was deeply in debt,[3] and needed the return of his estates and mines in order to satisfy his creditors. He also treated for a free pardon, for the normal practice was to impose a heavy fine and to sequester the estates of active Royalists. In July 1647, the Lords and Commons resolved that his terms should be accepted :

> That upon delivery up of the Isle of Lundy to the Lord Viscount Saye and Seale or his assigns, by Mr Thomas Bushell, the delinquency of the said Thomas Bushell be taken off, and all Sequestration in respect thereof be discharged; and he (be) restored to such Right as he or his Assigns had or ought to have in the mines of Devonshire, Wales or Cornwall, and to all other his estates and rights whatsoever; and that the men that were with him in the Island, being not soldiers of Estate and fortune, be pardoned and freed from delinquencie.[4]

Upon receipt of this assurance, Bushell surrendered the island to Lord Saye and Sele's son and retired to London.

After the execution of King Charles, Lord Saye and Sele withdrew from public life in protest, and settled on Lundy. Parliament was concerned that the island should be in such equivocal hands, and sent their own agent and a file of musketeers to safeguard it.

On the restoration, Bushell petitioned for his expenses in maintaining and garrisoning the island for the King, and was supported by John Grenville, Earl of Bath, to whom the island had then reverted. Bushell eventually received £2,000, but when he died, it was found that he was £120,000 in debt. With the coming of more settled times, Lundy was left to the pirates again.

In 1663 it was reported to the Admiralty that a French pirate had made Lundy his base, and later, that three more were skulking under the lee of the island. These were said to have seized six barques bound for Bideford, and to have sent onshore demands for a ransom for the crews. Fears were also entertained that the Dutch would make the island a base for their operations against the British coast. However, politics decreed that the Dutch should become allies in the struggle against Louis XIV, and this led to a successful ruse being played off on the island. A French privateer anchored off the coast and, pretending to be Dutch, landed on Lundy to ask for some fresh milk for their sick captain. The trusting inhabitants were only too happy to be of assistance, and the request was repeated for several days with the same response. Finally, the crew, with simulated grief, asked permission to bury the captain in the island cemetery in the presence of all the islanders. This was agreed, and the crew carried the coffin up to the chapel. Asking the natives to wait outside, the 'Dutchmen' armed themselves from a supply concealed in the coffin and then fell upon their dupes, making prisoners of them all. They then seized the livestock, throwing most of it into the sea, and stripped the inhabitants of their valuables, even down to their clothing. Guns and fortifications were destroyed until finally, satiated with plunder and destruction, they sailed away, leaving ruin and desolation behind them. Lundy's pirate connection even included the notorious Captain Kidd, although fortunately he was a prisoner when brought to the island in 1700 by his captors to await instructions on his disposal.

In the early 1700s, Lundy passed from the Grenvilles to Lord Gower who granted it by lease to a prominent Bideford merchant, Thomas Benson, who was to leave lasting mark of his tenure. Benson had inherited a fortune of £40,000, and had been Sheriff of Devonshire. In 1747 he was elected to Parliament as the member for Barnstaple, and soon afterwards made a contract with the government to carry convicts abroad to the penal colonies of Virginia and Maryland. However, on obtaining Lundy the following year, he landed his convicts there and employed them on building and farming. Whether this was the purpose for which he acquired the island is not known, but they were certainly put to good use there. For many years he persisted in this practice undiscovered, until, becoming overconfident, he invited a party of visitors to the island who not only reported the presence of the convicts but also that Benson regarded Lundy as his own private kingdom and fired a gun at any ship that did not render passing honours to his state. Benson's ingenuous explanation of the convicts was that 'sending them to Lundy was the same as sending them to America; they were transported from England, it mattered not where it was, so long as they were out of the Kingdom'.[5]

Benson was also engaged in smuggling, and it was the discovery of this that finally caused his downfall. He was fined £5,000 and deprived of his offices, and when he failed to pay and remained on Lundy, the Sheriff of Devon was obliged to go there and, in lieu of payment, seized tobacco and other goods that Benson had concealed on the island. As the value of these still did not clear the fine, Benson's estate near Bideford was also seized. Meanwhile, Benson had perpetrated the greatest outrage of all. He had heavily insured the cargo of one of his ships, the *Nightingale*, and then arranged that it should put in to Lundy and land its cargo of pewter, linen and salt, which was hidden on the island. When the vessel put to sea again, the master set it on fire and abandoned it. The crew were picked up and landed at Bideford, where they swore that the fire had been accidently caused. However, one of the crew later let the cat out of the bag, and the master and first mate were prosecuted for attempting to defraud. Benson fled to Portugal to avoid arrest, leaving his fellow conspirators to face the music. The master was hanged for his part in the plot, but Benson managed to survive the storm, and died in Portugal in 1772.

Meanwhile, Lundy's owner, Earl Gower, had died in 1754, and for twenty years his executors were unable to find a buyer for Lundy. At last, it was bought by the young MP for Marlow, Sir John Borlase Warren, for only £510. He is reported to have lived on Lundy during his ownership, and he it was who built the original and oldest part of the present hotel buildings. He made an attempt to settle some Irishmen, but this was a failure, and the Irish are remembered only for their removal of timber from the castle for firewood. Warren spent upwards of £6,000 in building his house and in completing the walls begun by Benson's convicts, and also in starting to build a quay. At the outbreak of the American War of Independence in 1776 he sold his yacht and gave up Lundy in order to volunteer for sea service. Some time later, the island was sold to John Cleveland for £1,200. Descriptions of the island at this time are given in Appendix D.

In 1794, there were seven houses and twenty-three inhabitants on the island. The buildings included, besides the castle and the chapel, a house near St Helen's Well where a brewhouse was being built, a watch-tower near the landing-place and another at North End. Two walls had been completed, South Wall and Halfway Wall. There were several forts on the island, armed with six small and one large cannon. These were all surveyed by the military during the invasion scares on the outbreak of war with France.

It may have been this fear of the French invasion, or of government requisition, that caused a remarkable depreciation in the value of Lundy. The story goes that a Sir Vere Hunt, during a walk in London, happened to pass an auction-room where a sale was in progress. Attracted by the noise, he went in and heard the auctioneer declaiming in glowing terms the advantages of owning Lundy. 'It never paid tax or tithe, acknowledged neither King nor Parliament, nor law civil or ecclesiastical, and that its proprietor was Pope and Emperor at once in his scanty domain.' Attracted, no doubt, by this econimum, Hunt had the island knocked down to him for £700.[6]

Hunt died in 1818, and left Lundy to his son. Just after his death, the long projected lighthouse was built on Beacon Hill by Trinity House. The son soon gambled away his inheritance, staking the island for £4,500 in a game of cards. He lost, and the new owners, suddenly finding themselves in possession of an island they did not want, hurriedly set about finding a purchaser for their unexpected acquisition.

In 1834 they succeeded in selling Lundy for £9,870 to William Hudson Heaven, who was to own it during one of the island's most prosperous periods. He made Lundy his home, and that of his family, for over eighty years. From his childhood days in Bristol, William Heaven had cherished an ambition to own an island, and when his fortunes were such that he could turn this dream into a reality, he first considered an island in the St Lawrence River. He was advised against this, and recommended to buy Lundy for the wild-game shooting. Heaven was well satisfied with his purchase, and at once set about improving the island. In 1836 he built Millcombe in the valley of the same name, having decided against Gannet's Combe as a possible site. The completion of the house was a considerable achievement as he had to import all the materials for building, as well as his furniture, into the island and have them dragged up the steep track from the beach by sleds pulled by donkeys and oxen. Heaven did not remain long satisfied with this rude means of transport and approached Trinity House with a view to a joint undertaking to build a road suitable for wheeled traffic up from the beach. When Trinity House engineers declared the task impossible, Heaven went ahead on his own, designing the road himself, and it was eventually constructed to join up with the existing Trinity House road on the plateau. Living as resident landlord, he was able to supervise many other improvements at the same time.

In 1840, a newspaper announced that Lundy was to be put up for sale, and gave the following glowing description of its attractions:

> . . . the mansion is of recent creation and combines within it all the accommodation 'a patriotic little monarch' can desire with corresponding offices of every description. Where shall ambition find such solace in all its lofty pretensions? Amid this scene of quiet repose and perfect independence two of the most favoured sea-bathing establishments are all but in view. An excellent farmhouse has recently been built with Kyanised timber and slated roof and there are six superior cottages close by. A great part of

the island is let with this farm for seven years at an exceedingly low rent but the great source of revenue is yet to be divulged : First 'the extensive fishery' without fear of any rival, especially for herrings and lobsters, which must produce an incalculably large income. The granite throughout the island in the hands of an enterprising man will realise a fortune; the minerals including silver and copper have been discovered near the beach. The sporting over the demesne undisturbed by Mortal Man is of the highest order and during the season myriads of little seabirds pay their annual visit and become tributary to the island by depositing countless of their eggs and dropping their beautiful feathers, all of which become a source of income. The Woodcock, Snipe and Wildfowl shooting is not surpassable anywhere . . . the Government is to form a 'Harbour of Refuge' and Nature seems to have pointed out its eligibility for such a God-like purpose . . . the land is adapted to create a Capital Pottery . . . the turmoil of politics will not intrude to distract the harmony of the little Monarch of the Isle; happiness, contentment and independence will be as firmly fixed as the rock on which the island is placed. Communication from Bristol and Tenby is almost daily.

Despite all this, Mr Heaven was left in possession, and in 1849 Charles Kingsley was describing a visit there : '. . . We dined at the Farmhouse, dinner costing me 1s 9d, and then rambled over the island . . . O that I had been a painter for that day at least !' As this was Kingsley's only visit to the island, it must have been the occasion on which he gathered the material for his description of it in *Westward Ho!*

In 1852, the government considered the possible use of Lundy for the detention of criminals, an idea which had several times previously been put forward without regard to the wishes of the owners. There are no further records of the island being offered for sale until 1906, so it is evident that Heaven decided to develop the commercial possibilities of his property himself. The Lundy Granite Co Ltd was set up in 1863 and flourished for five years. The directors imported 300 workers, which caused an acute housing shortage that was only remedied by the building of bunkhouses and cottages. A hospital was also built. When the company got into difficulties and was wound up in 1868, the equipment was sold but the last employees did not leave until 1887, when the lease rights reverted back to the Heaven family.

Other ventures followed, which will be discussed more fully in Chapter 8, but none was really successful, and the island farm was again leased to tenants in 1875. One enterprising tenant started the hotel in part of the farmhouse, a business that has continued ever since.

William Hudson Heaven died in 1883 and was succeeded by his son, the Rev Hudson Grosett Heaven, who achieved a long-standing ambition to build a new church on the island. Work started in 1896, using stone from Quarter Wall village, and the building was dedicated to St Helena in 1897. At about the same time Trinity House built new lighthouses at either end of Lundy, and the original one on Beacon Hill was abandoned. The light-houses were built of granite from the neglected quarries, and for a few months the island was invaded by workmen again. Further attempts were subsequently made to revive the quarries, but there were few takers for the subscriptions. Later, the entire island was let on lease, and the hotel business was expanded by the tenants.

Lundy became headline news in 1906, when the first-class battleship HMS *Montagu* ran aground near Shutter Rock. Salvage operations continued on her until 1922.

The island was again in the market in 1906, and an eccentric clergyman, under the mistaken impression that he would acquire salvage rights and ownership of the wrecked battleship, offered £30,000, which was provisionally accepted. Previously, the Rev Hudson Heaven had declined an offer from a Continental baron to establish an island Monte Carlo, firmly stating that 'he had no intention of allowing Lundy to be turned into a gambling hell.' Private negotiations having come to nothing, the island was put up for auction but did not make the reserve price of £25,000, and was withdrawn. The Rev Mr Heaven remained on the island until his retirement in 1911, when it was advertised for sale in *Country Life*. Again, there were no takers and in 1916 it passed to his nephew, Walter Heaven.

During the first world war, Lundy was virtually uninhabited. The Heaven family moved to the mainland on the declaration of war, leaving only the farmer and the Trinity House staff on the island. German submarines were soon active in the Bristol Channel, and, an example of the cycles of history, there were rumours that Lundy was being used as a German rendezvous. In 1915, an MP with an exaggerated view of the available accommodation suggested that the island should be used as a prisoner-of-war camp, stating that the buildings in repair could accommodate 1,600 prisoners, and that the derelict quarry buildings could soon be converted to hold many more. Fortunately, his suggestion was not adopted.

Walter Heaven was obliged to sell the island in 1917 and the buyer, Mr Augustus Langham Christie, was a descendant of the John Cleveland who had bought it some 130 years previously. The new owner soon leased out the land, the hotel was reopened, and Millcombe redecorated with a view to its use as a second hotel, though this idea later fell through. Christie built a slipway in the cove, which he planned to use in conjunction with the *Lerina*, the Lundy boat.

The island was sold again eight years later to Mr Martin Coles Harman for £16,000, plus an ingoing valuation of £9,250, which included the *Lerina*. Mr Harman will be remembered especially for his work in founding the Lundy Field Society, of which he became the first president, in 1947. An enthusiastic naturalist, he allowed the society to use the Old Light and its outbuildings, and took a personal and sustained interest in their work. At various times he introduced new species of animals to Lundy, and evolved the distinct breed of Lundy pony, which has had considerable success. He also introduced the well-known Puffin coins and Lundy stamps in 1929.

During the second world war Lundy became a base for naval patrol vessels, and a detachment of six signallers and one officer was maintained at the Old Light. In 1944, Mr Harman's eldest son was killed in action and awarded a posthumous Victoria Cross. Mr Harman himself died in 1954, and Lundy then be-

Page 71 : *(above)* Transporting supplies from the beach about 1900; *(below)* fishermen at the foot of the slipway about 1900

Page 72: (above) Signal rocket at Battery, used between 1863 and 1897; (below) copy of photographic illustration issued with prospectus of Lundy Island & Mainland Quarries Limited, 1899

came the joint property of his surviving sons and daughters, Mr A. P. Harman, Mrs R. Harman-Jones, and Mrs D. Keast.

Lundy entertained its first royal visitor on 11 May 1958, when Her Majesty, Queen Elizabeth the Queen Mother, spent two and a half hours ashore there on her way back from a visit to Northern Ireland. Islanders and guests were presented to her, and she was graciously pleased to sign an illuminated vellum to commemorate her visit.

On the untimely death of Mr A. P. Harman in June 1968 his third share of the island passed to his widow, and in March of the following year the three joint owners reluctantly decided to offer the island for sale, with possession by September 1969. An auction for the property was due to take place on 18 July and among those who were expected to bid were the Scientologists, seeking a rest home for their members, and several Americans possibly attracted by the island's reputation as a tax-free haven— despite the auctioneers' conditions of sale which made it clear that the Crown still claimed jurisdiction over Lundy.

The National Trust was anxious to buy the island but saw little likelihood of being able to find the minimum price of £100,000. Then in May, from a clear sky, Mr Jack Hayward, a 46-year-old British property developer from the Bahamas, telephoned Mr Jeremy Thorpe, the Liberal leader and one of an all-party action committee of West Country MPs seeking to safeguard Lundy, to say that he would like to present the island to the nation in gratitude for all that Britain had done for him. He donated the purchase price of £150,000 to the National Trust which, on 22 May 1969, was able to announce that it had acquired Lundy and that the responsibility for running it would be in the hands of the Landmark Trust, a body set up in 1965 to protect and restore buildings or areas of special national interest. The Landmark Trust, under the chairmanship of Mr John Smith, Conservative MP for the Cities of London and Westminster, whose family set up the trust, were granted a sixty-year lease of the island at a peppercorn rent and a public appeal

E

73

was then launched by the West Country MPs for £75,000 to restore buildings and carry out improvements.

When Mr Hayward visited the island for the first time on 6 July 1969, a scroll of thanks signed by each of the ten permanent inhabitants was presented to him by the seventy-nine-year-old agent, Mr Felix Gade, a resident on Lundy since 1926, and the Union Jack was run up on the island flagstaff. Thus, chiefly through the generosity and patriotism of Mr Hayward, the preservation of Lundy as an unspoilt place of great natural beauty and historic interest is assured.

5   THE CASTLE

THE castle is one of the most interesting survivals of the island's history, and although it is known as Marisco Castle it was, in fact, constructed by Henry III after the downfall of the de Mariscos. Immediately after gaining possession of Lundy in 1242, Henry determined to fortify the island to prevent it ever again falling into the hands of his enemies. Work began in 1243 to build a 'stone fort', which consisted of a small, square keep, a system of outer walls, and a fosse. The site of the castle was well-chosen as it commanded not only the sole path to the plateau, but also the landing beach and the Bristol Channel.

The keep is roughly square, although it has undergone many alterations during its seven hundred years of existence. Rising sheer to the battlements, the original building was almost certainly on two floors. The south-west wall is 51 ft long, and the north-west wall is 38 ft. The stonework was simple and strictly functional. Although the original interior has entirely disappeared, it is thought that there was a cross wall, probably pierced by arches, supporting the upper floor and roof. The original slit windows have also disappeared, but the doorway, which was about 8 ft high, can still be traced in the centre of the south-east wall, and in front of it are the foundations of a building, a flight of stairs, and a small parade, on which were mounted five guns.

The outer fortification walls can still be followed, and the fosse which once surrounded them is very evident just north of the keep, although its extent and original depth is still a matter for conjecture. There would have been two gates piercing the outer walls, one to the north of the keep at the head of the beach path, and the other to the west giving access to the plateau. A piped water supply leading from a spring in the Lighthouse field was

75

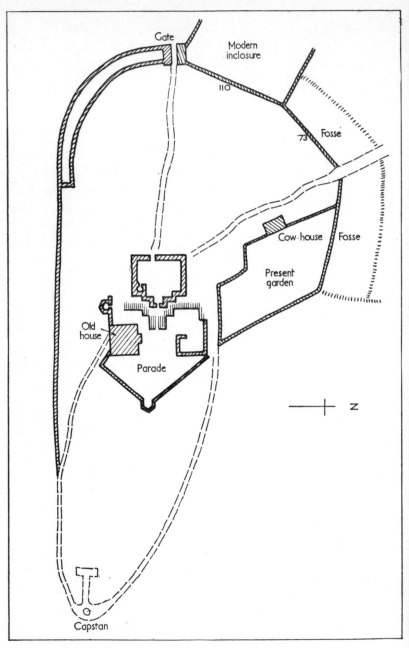

Marisco castle plan showing location. (After Grose, 1776)

discovered near the summit of Castle Hill in 1936, and is thought to date from the original building of the castle.

The castle keep is the oldest remaining building on the island, and, until the building of the hotel complex, was the principal residence. The buildings must have deteriorated considerably by the time that Thomas Bushell arrived to garrison the island for Charles I, for he claimed £5,570 for 'maintaining Lundy garrison and building the castle . . . from the ground at his own charge, fit for any noble person to inhabit'. When Sir Aubrey de Vere Hunt introduced Irish labourers to Lundy in the early nineteenth century, they were housed in the castle and destroyed 'all the remaining woodwork, and amongst other things, the old entrance gates and posts which had been placed there at the time when the castle was prepared for the refuge of Edward II.'

About 1850, the need for accommodation for the fishermen became acute, and the keep, by this time a hollow shell, was used to enclose three cottages facing a small central courtyard. The remains of the original doors and windows were blocked up, and the walls at the west corner extended to afford some protection. All that now remains are the shells of the cottages, the overgrown cobbled courtyard and the half-buried steps leading down to it.

Two habitable buildings remain, both of recent origin. The cottage at the head of the beach path was built between 1902 and 1903 by a fisherman for £150, and was then known as the 'Palace'. In 1963 it was rebuilt, and is now known as 'Hanmers', after the family who used it as a holiday cottage. The stone hut against the north-east wall of the keep was built in 1887 to house the terminal of the telegraph cable, and then consisted of one room and a lobby. In 1960, the walls were raised and extended to form the present Castle Cottage, which, like Hanmers, is available for letting to summer visitors. The small hut on the castle parade was built as a lookout by Lloyd's, and has been renovated to provide additional sleeping accommodation for Castle Cottage. In 1906–8 the Admiralty had built the two cottages, with the attached lookout, to the west of the castle which are now in ruins, and in 1909 took over the two adjacent cottages which had belonged to Lloyd's.

From the parade in front of the castle, the ground slopes down steeply, and two grassy paths converge at the entrance of Benson's Cave. This is an underground cavern which is believed to have been used by Benson to store the goods he obtained by piracy and smuggling. The cement used in the cave is identical to that used in the older parts of the castle, and it is probable that it was originally built by Bushell, who was a mining engineer. If Bushell did rebuild the castle as he claimed, the cave would have been an ideal place for his mint—the metals and coins could have been stored there with safety, and the cave mouth would have been large enough to house the furnace and presses. Remembering that Bushell must have pursued his coining expecting at any moment to be beseiged, and that he had already been chased away from his previous bases, it would be quite natural that he should wish to carry on his activities with the maximum degree of security.

Markings and inscriptions on the roof and walls bear out the belief that the cave was later used to house Benson's convicts, and possibly contraband as well. There was once a capstan mounted in the cave mouth which could have been used to haul goods up from the beach. At the cave mouth there are two recesses which have had a brick facing and a doorway added to convert them into two chambers.

Although the castle is now in very poor condition, and its landward aspect is marred by the modern buildings nearby, the keep nevertheless remains most impressive, and, when seen from the landing cove, still retains a striking grandeur.

6 COMMUNICATIONS

TODAY, communications between the island and the mainland are extremely good—fifteen minutes by air from the mainland, and a regular service by water, taking an average of three hours for the crossing. Before Mr Heaven's ownership, however, Lundy was as remote as anywhere in the United Kingdom, with no regular communications at all. Passage to the island could be obtained only by striking a bargain with one of the fishermen from the mainland to take passengers out, and also getting them to call again when persons wished to be taken off. The weather, of course, had a great effect on the willingness or otherwise of the fishermen to oblige, and many times must Lundy have been out of all touch with the mainland.

The coming of the Trinity House settlement strengthened the contacts with the shore, and the earliest recorded regular visitor was the lighthouse tender *Ranger*, which came into service in 1857. Sailings were made from Clovelly every Friday morning early, and the crew of two brought across the mail, which was collected once a week. Mr Heaven owned a schoolroom yacht, *Lady of the Isle*, which was capable of carrying passengers and stores across if needed. The only other vessel to visit Lundy with any regularity was a coaster, which called every ten days to collect fish for the London market from about 1869. The granite company ran an irregular service from Instow in a small steamer.

Between 1871 and 1878 various ships were chartered to carry the mails, but from 1878 onwards the *Gannet* acted as the island boat, and only very occasionally was it necessary to charter other boats to carry cargoes of coal or lime that were too bulky for the *Gannet*. On the island itself, Walter Heaven built the little sailing boat *Heatherbell* in 1886–7, and made many crossings in her during the summer months.

79

A notice in Ward's *North Devon* in 1885 described the *Gannet* service :

> The wooden skiff *Gannet* of 40 tons, one of the smartest boats in the Channel, makes the journey to and fro on alternate Thursdays, and starts from Instow Quay . . . single fare 5s; return 7s 6d. Captain Dark . . . charges 30s for the use of his skiff on other than mail days. . . . On arriving as well as on leaving a careful count is made of the number of visitors, as no 'stowaways' are allowed on the island.

By 1903, mail sailings were made every Thursday, and a guide book of 1907 mentions that the fares were reduced to 2s 6d each way, and also that a private sailing-boat could be hired from Clovelly for 25s return.

The *Gannet* later operated a twice-weekly service until 1921 when Mr Christie bought the 71-ton Lowestoft drifter *Lerina*. For a short while, both boats were used, but in 1923 the *Gannet* crossed the Bideford Bar for the last time, with her successor as escort. The *Lerina* was built in 1917, and for the Lundy service was equipped with two 16-ft lifeboats on davits to enable her to carry forty passengers as well as her crew of three. After a few months, however, it became obvious that the ship was not suited to carry such heavy lifeboats, and these were dispensed with, the passenger load being reduced to twelve. The journey between Instow and Lundy took three hours.

During the second world war, the *Lerina* was first lent and then sold to the Admiralty, but was bought back in 1946 when, under Captain G. Wilson, she resumed the Lundy services. During the war, a Belgian trawler, *Der Helige Familje*, was used to supply the island. When the *Lerina* returned, she remained in use until 1950, but as she became increasingly troublesome and unseaworthy, was finally laid up in 1950. She was beached at Bideford and an attempt was made to auction her in 1954, but she failed to make even £1 and was later broken up.

Between 1950 and 1956, regular transport to Lundy depended on the air service, which had been started in 1934. The service was operated from the North Devon aerodrome at Chivenor by the Lundy & Atlantic Coast Airlines, using a Short 'Scion' five-seater cabin monoplane and a three-seater cabin 'Monospar'. Initially, a twice-daily service was operated from April to September, with a weekly flight in winter. The return fare was 17s 6d, and the flights continued until the outbreak of war, when private flying was suspended and Chivenor airfield was taken over by the Royal Air Force.

At the end of the war, the RAF allowed civilian aircraft to use part of the much enlarged airfied, and flights to Lundy were resumed at the end of 1950 by a company called Devon Air Travel, using a DH 'Rapide' twin-engined biplane. In 1953 this company was succeeded by Devonair, which ran a regular service using single-engined Austers. The service never became fully economic, and was eventually withdrawn.

Early in 1956, Mr Albion Harman bought a fishing vessel *The Pride of Scarborough*, which was given a thorough overhaul and had new diesel engines fitted. She was renamed the *Lundy Gannet* and, after a short service of dedication at Bideford quay, made her maiden voyage to Lundy in 1956. Licensed to carry a crew of four and twelve passengers, she is normally manned by two crew and crosses once a week in winter and three times a week in the summer season, carrying passengers, mail, stores, and livestock. It is now rarely necessary to charter larger vessels to carry heavy equipment or large numbers of livestock.

Apart from the regular services, Lundy has been visited by excursion steamers since at least 1870. At one time there was acute competition between rival companies, and inducements in the form of 'minstrel bands' were held out to prospective passengers. Now only the White Funnel fleet of P. & A. Campbell provides steamer excursions to Lundy from Bristol Channel ports during summer. Passengers are landed on the island by motor launches, which are moored there during the season and manned by the company's employees, who live in one of the island cottages for the summer.

From the very earliest times, Lundy's value as shelter from westerly gales has been recognised by mariners, and the roads on the east side became a frequent resort for sailing ships sheltering from adverse weather. In the nineteenth century, the volume of shipping using the Bristol Channel grew so large that a select committee of the House of Commons was set up, which suggested that a harbour of refuge should be built on Lundy. Two years later, a royal commission reported that, although the site would be ideal, the estimated cost would be prohibitive at £3 million. The scheme envisaged the building of a breakwater some mile and threequarters long, enclosing an area of about 714 acres. Apart from the cost, other disadvantages were the frequent fogs, the tricky tide races, and the total lack of repair facilities.

As the volume of shipping continued to grow—an estimated million vessels passed Lundy in 1876—the plans were reconsidered and a simpler construction, using convict labour, was proposed in 1874. The report mentions that Mr Heaven was prepared to sell the island for £40,000, and that :

> . . . a Harbour of Refuge at Lundy Island would afford shelter with less risk than any other place. A port of departure from which vessels could get to sea with the first favourable start of wind, large vessels could be towed down from Cardiff, Gloucester and Bristol etc. It is also well situated for the collection of convoys and for a Naval station to watch the Channel. Being subject to no violence from the sea to the eastward, a breakwater would be of the cheapest description, a mere rubble mound, the construction of which requiring little skilled labour, would be well adapted for the employment of convicts for the safe custody of whom the island would afford every facility. . . . In 1879 the number of vessels that left the several ports in the Bristol Channel amounted to 39,329 containing 5,634,294 tons of iron and coal, showing that upwards of 78,000 vessels pass and repass Lundy Island in a year amounting to one-sixth of the entire shipping of the United Kingdom. . . . There can be no doubt that if the proposed Harbour of Refuge and Convict station should meet the approval of the present government and be carried out as recommended it would prove one of the greatest national benefits of the age in rendering most valuable assistance to the Mercantile interests of all nations as also the saving of life and property. The Convict staff and establishment at Portland could be transferred to Lundy Island as

the Harbour of Refuge at Portland is now complete which would prevent additional cost to the country beyond the expense of erecting suitable prisons and barracks.

These proposals were discussed for some years, much as the Channel Tunnel scheme has been in recent times, but despite strong recommendations, nothing was ever done.

Steps were taken, however, to establish a reporting station in communication with the mainland for the purpose of informing Lloyd's, or owners, when their ships were delayed in the roads. Previously, the existing means of contact in bad weather had been by bonfire or heliograph. Proposals for a cable from Lundy had been made as early as 1870, but work did not begin seriously until 1883, and the first telegraphic link was made to Hartland Point in the subsequent year. The telegraph was manned by employees of Lloyd's, who opened the telegraph office daily from 8 am to 10 pm. The two signal-station cottages were built for them in 1885, and a small hut was erected on the castle parade, remaining in use until 1909 when the Tibbett's Hill station was built for the Admiralty coastguards. The cable had been financed privately, and was not a commercial success, for the rocky sea-bed near Hartland broke the cable on several occasions, and the excessively heavy cost of repairs led to its abandonment in 1887.

That the harbour of refuge idea was not altogether neglected was shown by the concern of the merchants of Bristol for the shale saddle which protects the landing bay. They offered to subscribe £8,000 to reinforce it and, somewhat later, a party of notables from Bristol and Swansea visited Lundy in 1888 to inspect the site. The usual Victorian junketings marked this visit, the police band being in attendance, and fifty sat down to a 'sumptuous repast', which seemed to be then inseparable from such occasions. Not unnaturally, the conclusion arrived at was that Lundy was ideal for a harbour!

Meanwhile, the island was still without telegraphic links with the shore, and it was not until 1893 that the GPO installed a line from Croyde Bay to terminate in a hut which was built against the castle. On the inauguration of the new cable, Mr Heaven sent the first message—'The Kingdom of Heaven rejoiceth'. The same sad story continued with this cable, however, starting with a surprising break four miles out from Croyde, where the seabed was sand. Subsequently the cable repeatedly parted, on one occasion so close to Lundy that it was suspected that it had been deliberately cut after a ship's anchor had fouled it. Repairs were usually made immediately, but when the cable broke in 1917, work was not started until two years later.[1] After two breakages in 1928, the GPO closed the post office and cable station, and left the cable unrepaired. Mr Harman undertook to carry the mails for the GPO, which relieved the Post Office of a considerable burden, since the revenue accruing from the island was very small.

Once again Lundy had no direct link with the shore, and concern was expressed for the shipping. At that time, the marine department of the Board of Trade was responsible for safety at sea, and Mr Harman entered into an agreement with them to install a Marconi radio telephone and to be responsible for watching the coasts of Lundy. The Board of Trade, for their part, installed a similar set at the coastguard station at Hartland Point, and it was arranged that the coastguards would transmit private messages as well as those concerned with shipping. It was further agreed that the GPO would allow the Lundy transmitter to be operated by someone who had not taken the GPO examination. The Lundy coastguard station was closed down following this in 1928, and the operator on Lundy still holds the unique position of uncertificated wireless operator. The original transmitter was replaced by a naval TV5 set in 1945, and operated at least twice a day from the hotel on a wavelength of 183 metres.

Internal communications were improved in 1910 by the installation of a telephone system running the entire length of the island, connecting the north and south lighthouses with Tibbett's station. Subsequently, the Old Light and the hotel were joined to this system, but in 1966 the Old Light connection was transferred to Stoneycroft, where the deputy-agent lives.

COMMUNICATIONS

The disused telegraph cable, lying broken about a mile from Lundy, was bought by Mr Harman for the token sum of 2s 6d, and remains *in situ* along the rocks of the beach as a link with the past and a reminder of the many times that Lundy's communications with the outside world have been broken.

7 WRECKS AND LIGHTHOUSES

BECAUSE of its position astride the sea routes to Bristol and the coastal ports of the Channel, it was inevitable that Lundy should have had a long history of shipwreck and marine disaster. Many a desperate drama has been played out on the rocky coast, and small chance of survival existed for the unfortunate vessels cast against the steep cliffs.

The first recorded wreck was that of the *Wye*, which was built at Chepstow in 1796 and lost on Lundy the same year, when 'every soul perished'. In the early part of the next year, a valuable cargo of gold dust and ivory was lost when the three-masted Bristol schooner *Jenny* was wrecked on the West Side, a site known ever since as Jenny's Cove. Attempts were made at salvage, and though the ivory was partially recovered, the gold dust, shipped in leather bags, had been washed away.

In 1813 Lundy was the scene of one of the actions in the American war. The second Leeward Island Fleet was homeward bound up-Channel in a thick fog. The fog lifted, and the US brig *Argus* discovered herself sailing in the middle of a fleet of eleven hostile ships of war. In the ensuing action, she managed to account for one vessel, the *Mariner*, which caught fire and was burnt out.

Many an unknown ship sank off the coasts, and usually only a laconic epitaph survives; in 1825, for example, the burial-ground records show 'several shipwrecked mariners were interred'. Sometimes a ship managed to cheat the rocks, as happened to the barque *Abbotsford*, which was driven ashore in 1836, but was later refloated and taken to Ilfracombe for repairs. In 1838, William Yeo of Bideford gave a graphic report to the royal commissioners of the perils of being anchored on a lee shore : 'We managed to get our anchors, but a ship belonging to Shields which lay alongside of us could not. She went ashore and went to pieces.' In the days of sail, sudden changes of wind, such as are not uncommon in the Bristol Channel, could in a moment convert a refuge into a death trap, and fortunate was the mariner who could up anchor and claw his way against the wind to the open sea and safety.

The pilots, then as now, were in the forefront of the efforts made to save life at sea and to render the coasts safe for shipping. In 1849, the US ship *Archelaus*, outward bound from Cardiff to New York, sank in the Lundy Roads. For their efforts in saving all twenty-two members of the crew, three Pill pilots were later awarded £5 each.

From 1850, until the first world war, an annual register of wrecks was published, which gave full details of most of the marine accidents around the coasts of Britain. The first Lundy record appears on the second day of the establishment of the register, when an unknown barque sank in the roads with the loss of four lives. For some months, the Lundy record contains details of the wrecks of anonymous vessels, many a vessel being found on the shore with no survivors to amplify the bare details of the tragedy. The record is occasionally incomplete, for from 1852 no wrecks are listed for six years, although details have survived from other sources, such as the local newspapers. A report in one such paper for 1856 states that a party of divers were :

> . . . exerting their skill, aided by the appliances of science but hitherto without any decided success in raising the precious things from the sunken vessels around this island. The *Loire* steamer sunk some time ago as she was on her voyage from Cardiff to Rouen, laden with coals, still lies snugly in custody of Davy Jones . . . her whereabouts is now difficult to find; the masts which served as a buoy having been washed away by the action of the sea. The *Avon*, which drifted and sank on the north-west side about twelve months since (*ie* in 1855) laden with copper ore from Cuba, still remains in the dark.

Some weeks later, the same paper reported that two tons of copper ore had been recovered from the total of 560 carried by the *Avon*. So the list runs on, with disasters due to fog, storms, high winds and, sometimes, sheer incompetence. Only occasionally do we learn more than the bare facts of the tragedies, as in this account of the wreck of the *Hannah Moore* on Rat Island in 1866 with the loss of nineteen of her crew of twenty-five.[1]

The 1,129-ton ship had arrived in Lundy Roads two days previously with a cargo of guano. On Wednesday night, a great gale began to blow and the wind chopped to every quarter in hurricane force. The *Hannah Moore* attempted to set her canvas to beat off the shore, but her sails were blown to fragments. She began to drag and one cable parted. The ship swung broadside to the seas and her decks were swept of everything. In the first gleam of morning, those on the shore saw the crew clinging to the lower rigging. A rescue was organised by a young surgeon on a visit to the island. Two Bideford men, Thomas Saunders and Samuel Jarman, went out in Mr Heaven's small punt and made two attempts to take out a line . . . a giant wave lifted the ship on to Rat Island on her side and in twenty minutes she had disintegrated. All but six of the crew were washed off, but these six remained on a portion of the rock from daylight until 4 pm. After five attempts to reach them in the small punt they were at length brought back to the beach. The remainder were seen clinging to spars and were carried by the eddy round Rat Island to the westward, where they drifted for hours to and fro in the currents before many of them were dashed against the rocks.

On a lighter note, a Genoese barque *Columbia* was once put ashore by her captain on the landing beach. He reported that to try and stop a leak he wanted to shift some of the cargo ashore at low tide. The crew went ashore for supplies, leaving one man, Agostino, in charge as anchor watch. He smelt burning, and on searching for the fire came upon pools of oil, which he believed had been deliberately poured on the timbers. Drizzling rain and the rising tide eventually combined to extinguish the flames, but the vessel was a total loss and, of course, it was subsequently discovered that ship and cargo had been heavily insured.

The toll continued to mount through the years as ship after

Page 89: (*left*) The Earthquake, showing depth of fissures; (*right*) interior of Benson's Cave

Page 90: (above) Construction of South Lighthouse in 1896; (below) South Lighthouse

ship went ashore on the island. In 1874, the smack *Fanny* went aground on the beach, and later broke up entirely. Her cargo of dressed granite can still be seen scattered on the beach. In 1882, all the crew of the brigantine *Heroine*, with the exception of the cook, were lost in particularly tragic circumstances. According to a contemporary report : [2]

> All the crew (of ten men) came ashore in their own boats and and scaled the cliffs at the north end of the island. All the effects belonging to the Captain and crew had to be abandoned. . . . On Friday morning (the day following) Captain Hirby and eight men left in a boat to save what small effects they could from the wreck, leaving the cook on the island with instructions to get dinner for them by their return, but up to the present time the unfortunate men have not returned, and the gravest fears are entertained that they have lost their lives. . . . Captain Bath states that he could not now see *Heroine* at all, and it is conjectured that she had backed off the rocks on which she rested and gone down in about fifteen fathoms of water, the poor fellows at the scene of the wreck going down with her or being swamped in their own boat.

In 1888, the steamship *Elsie* struck at Brazen Ward, and the attempts to save her caused the tenant farmer, Mr Wright, to complain to the Board of Trade that the island lacked any means of saving life. His plea resulted in the Board of Trade providing complete life-saving apparatus in 1893. However, before it arrived, a notable improvised feat of life-saving followed the wreck of the *Tunisie* of Bordeaux in 1892. This vessel struck the Sugar Loaf, and twenty-one Frenchmen were rescued by John McCarthy, one of the lighthouse keepers. He managed to send a line out to the ship by using an explosive fog-signal rocket to carry it out, and then brought the men ashore in an improvised breeches buoy made from an old coal bag. He was awarded 15s and the thanks of the RNLI inscribed on vellum as a reward.

Some idea of the dangers of Lundy may be gathered from the statistics issued by a royal commission of 1859, charged with reporting on the harbour of refuge scheme. They noted that 'out of 173 wrecks in the Bristol Channel in 1856–7, 97 received their damage and 44 lives were lost east of Lundy; while 76 vessels were lost or damaged and 58 lives sacrificed west of Lundy, thus showing the island to be nearly in the centre of the dangerous parts.' Later, at a meeting of Bideford council in 1904, it was stated that 'over 137 lives, roughly, had been lost in the Bristol Channel area in twelve months, but in October 1886 over 300 lives were lost "inside Lundy" and from 18–20 steamers foundered'.

Perhaps one of the most unfortunate, and certainly the most famous wreck to have occurred on Lundy was that of the first-class battleship HMS *Montagu*. This ship was launched in 1901, displaced 14,000 tons and had a complement of 750. She cost just over £1,000,000 complete. She was one of six ships in the Duncan class, named after famous admirals, and was described as a very handy and passable sea boat. In May 1906 she was serving with the Channel Fleet, and was testing new wireless equipment, when, in a thick fog, she struck a point to the north of Great Shutter Rock, fortunately without loss of life. The *Montagu* listed heavily to starboard, the wireless telegraphy equipment was shaken out of the rigging, and she was holed so that several compartments, including the engine-room, boiler-room and stokeholds were flooded. The Admiralty despatched her sister ships, *Duncan*, *Albemarle*, *Cornwallis* and *Exmouth*, together with a cruiser and several tugs, to the scene of the accident, and the Liverpool Salvage Association sent their salvage steamers *Ranger* and *Linnet*, 'with eight powerful steam pumps, a full equipment of salvage appliances and a large staff of divers under the command of Captain F. W. Young.' There were rumours that a floating dock was to be brought from Bermuda to receive the *Montagu* when she was refloated. The Commander-in-Chief arrived on 1 June with three ships and two lighters, and work at once began on removing as much as possible from *Montagu* to lighten her for refloating. But no sooner had one of the lighters been loaded with four six-inch guns and the torpedo nets, than it sank off the Rattles. It was hoped that the guns could be recovered on the spring ebb.

The salvage vessel *Ranger* arrived off Lundy at the end of August, and by this time it was clear that the battleship was a total wreck. Disagreements between the Admiralty salvage crews and the civilians led to the contract to salve what remained being given to the civil firm. The contractors landed a large party of workers on Lundy, where they lived during the operations. A wire rope suspension bridge was built from the island to the wreck, and a path was cut down the cliff, which is still known as the Montagu Steps. Of the ship nothing visible now remains, and the path has become dangerous.

The subsequent official report of the wreck was a fine blend of comedy and tragedy :

> . . . it was the opinion of the Officer Commanding that they had gone ashore at or near Hartland Point, and an officer and a small party of ratings was sent to investigate. Thinking they were south of Hartland Point, they rowed northwards, and landed below North Light, climbed up the very dangerous rock face and after much struggle reached the top. They then struck the path leading down to the North Light where they greatly astonished the keeper on duty by peering through the windows. So convinced was the officer that he had landed at Hartland that 'words passed', ending when the keeper assured him that he did really know which lighthouse he was in charge of.

This conversation weighed heavily against the commanding officer and his navigating officer at the court martial as proof of how far out they were in their reckoning. Both the captain and his navigator were severely reprimanded and dismissed their ship, the navigator losing two years' seniority. The captain retired with the rank of rear-admiral a few months later, and joined a shipbuilding firm.

In 1929, Mr M. C. Harman agreed with the Board of Trade to report shipping movements around Lundy, and to keep the rocket life-saving equipment in an efficient condition. He also arranged to carry out four drills a year with it, and to pay the rocket crew for drills and wreck services performed by them. Within two years the team was called out to save the crew of the Greek ship *Taxiarchis*, which was driven ashore at the quarries.

Mr Gade led a party of islanders who rescued the entire crew of twenty-four; the ship was refloated in 1933 and towed to the mainland for breaking up. The next big wreck occurred in 1937, when the *Carmine Filomena*, carrying coal to Genoa, struck near Rat Island. All the crew were saved, although the ship became a total wreck. Eleven days later, the *Nellie*, a Belgian ship just one month old, turned turtle after hitting the Hen and Chickens, and later a 12-ton yacht, the *Freckles*, hit the wreckage of the *Carmine Filomena* and sank.

The second world war led to a number of incidents, but with the advent of radar, the hazards around Lundy have been reduced. The Marisco tavern, however, is adorned with numerous reminders of the price exacted by the island from the unfortunate or the careless.

Over the years, efforts had been made to minimise the dangers of Lundy, and the first big step was taken in 1786, when a party of Bristol merchants offered to build a lighthouse on the island, and to maintain it at their own expense if the owner agreed to let them have a site. They decided that Beacon Hill was the best place, and in 1787 the foundations were laid. However, for one reason or another, work did not proceed until Trinity House obtained a 999-year lease of the site in 1819.

In 1807, Parliament had passed the Bristol Wharfage Act, and among the Act's provisions was an order that a pilotage service should be started for all vessels passing to the eastward of Lundy. The original procedure seems to have been for a pilot to join a ship sailing down Channel, and transfer at sea to a incoming ship. This system had obvious drawbacks, and at least one pilot had to remain with his charge all the way to New York. It seems likely that pilots were sometimes put ashore on Lundy to await an incoming vessel. In 1891, the compulsory pilotage area was reduced to the port of Bristol.

The Old Lighthouse was designed by Daniel Asher Alexander, one of the most important architects and civil engineers of his day, and was built of native granite by Joseph Nelson. Standing on the summit of Beacon Hill, 470 ft above sea level, the 97-ft

94

tower became the highest light in great Britain. Substantial quarters for the keepers were built adjoining the tower, and the whole work cost some £36,000. Two lights were provided, a broad steady beam shining to the west, and an upper revolving light with a range of 26 miles. The system was revolved by clockwork, and gave a flash every two minutes. The lower light consisted of a row of nine red lamps hung under a stone canopy, which can still be seen halfway up the west face of the tower; the lamps were visible over an arc of 90 degrees. The angle of the canopy was so arranged that the light was only visible to ships four miles or less from the shore. If the vessel did not alter course away from the island, the lights disappeared from sight, a warning that collision with the rocks was imminent.

It was found that, in practice, the red light merged with the upper light and, to counter this, the lamps were moved to a glass-fronted chamber at the foot of the tower. This solved that problem, but a greater remained. On a clear night, the light was visible for thirty miles, but it was frequently obscured by fog at the very time it was most needed. To try and obviate this, the Trinity House board obtained two Georgian 18-pounder cannon, which were installed at the base of the lighthouse to provide audible warning in fog. Later, the guns were established on the West Side cliffs, and a gunhouse and powder store constructed, together with two houses for the gun crews. During fog, a gun was fired every ten minutes. The tale is told of a ship's master approaching Lundy in dirty weather shortly after the guns had been installed, who remarked to his mate on the thunderstorms raging overhead and promptly ran ashore beneath the still-smoking guns. The guns are still in position today, although they are no longer in use.

Trinity House was still not satisfied with the arrangements during fog, and in 1878 substituted guncotton rockets for the guns. In 1881, the Elder Brethren considered moving the lower lights from the lighthouse to the battery; bells, hooters and whistles were tried, and plans put forward for a rocket station at the south of the island and a siren at the north. This last experiment was delayed for financial reasons, and was eventually shelved when it was decided to build two new lighthouses nearer sea level at either end of the island. These were started in 1896, and completed the following year, when the Old Light was used as a daymark only. The equipment from the Old Light was used, as far as possible, in the South Light, and the principal keeper's bungalow was also dismantled. The materials were taken by cart to Benson's Cave, just below the castle, where a wooden platform had been built, and from there it was carried out to the South Light by a cableway.

The lantern of the South Light is mounted on a 52-ft tower, 175 ft above sea level, and the original paraffin burner had a candle power of 40,000–60,000, flashed once a minute and was visible for nineteen miles. In 1925, the mechanism was modified to flash every half minute. The whole apparatus was replaced in 1962, when a new permanent electric light, powered by two 1,500-watt generators, was introduced. The 1,000-watt light is visible for twenty-two miles, and flashes for one-third of a second every five seconds. In fog, when rocks known as the Knoll Pins become invisible from the lighthouse, an electronic signal is sounded. Supplies to the tower are hauled up by a winch and fixed cable, originally powered by a steam donkey-engine which was replaced by a diesel in 1960.

The North Light is 4 ft higher than the South, standing 165 ft above high water. It cost £45,000 to build, and has a more modern boat-shaped reflector, which moves in a bath of mercury. In spite of its enormous weight, it moves so easily that a child could revolve it with one finger. It gives two white flashes every twenty seconds, and has a normal candle power of 81,000 and a maximum of 121,500. Powerful horns, driven by compressed air, are used during fog, and there is an automatic radio beacon which transmits a call sign every five minutes. The lighthouse is supplied by means of a narrow-gauge tramway, which runs there from the point where supplies are hauled up from the sea. All the water used is caught on the roof, and a goat is kept to supply fresh milk.

The lighthouses and the hotel are connected by telephone. Each lighthouse has a crew of four keepers, whose tour of duty is three months, followed by one month's leave. The working day is divided into periods of four hours on duty and eight hours off.

Lighthouses, radio beacons and radar have all made Lundy safer for navigators, but still the position of the island and tidal races athwart the shipping routes up the Channel make it a peril and a hazard to shipping. It is unlikely that the last entry has yet been made in the wreck logs of Lundy.

In the summer of 1969, a sea mine containing some 500 lb of high-explosive was found trapped between two rocks less than 200 yd from the landing beach. The mine was lying in about 20 ft of water and came to light as a result of activities by members of the diving school which operates from the island and plans, in time, to carry out an underwater inspection of every part of Lundy's coastline.

8 INDUSTRY

IT is difficult now to think of Lundy, with its lonely and distinctively island atmosphere, as having been the site of any industry other than agriculture, fishing, or catering for summer visitors. However, a number of companies have been formed in the past to exploit the natural resources of the island, and although none can be said to have been conspicuously successful, the granite industry lasted for some time and brought a little of the bustle of the outside world to the island.

The first, and most interesting, of the companies to be formed was the Lundy Granite Company, which left substantial traces of its activities that remain to this day. The objects of the company, which was registered in July 1863, were to open the quarries, to work and transport the granite from the island, and also to cultivate the farm. Provision was further made for the establishment of wharves at London or elsewhere, and for the general development of the resources of the entire island.

The original capital was £25,000, but this was later increased to £100,000, made up of 20,000 shares, of which 15,480 were taken up. However, the finances of the company were irregular, and when it was wound up in 1868, all the records were ordered to be sold as scrap, realising 30s for the benefit of the creditors. However, in its brief life the company opened and worked quarries on the East Side between Quarter Wall and Halfway Wall. The destruction of the official records has made it more difficult to form an idea of the methods of working the quarries, and field study has had to supplement the remaining eyewitness accounts, papers and maps. In 1962, the authors and Mr P. Cole were able to trace the routes of the quarry tramways and slipway, and to build up a clear picture of the workings.

The quarry workers were originally housed in wooden huts built near the present High Street farmyard. Later, they were

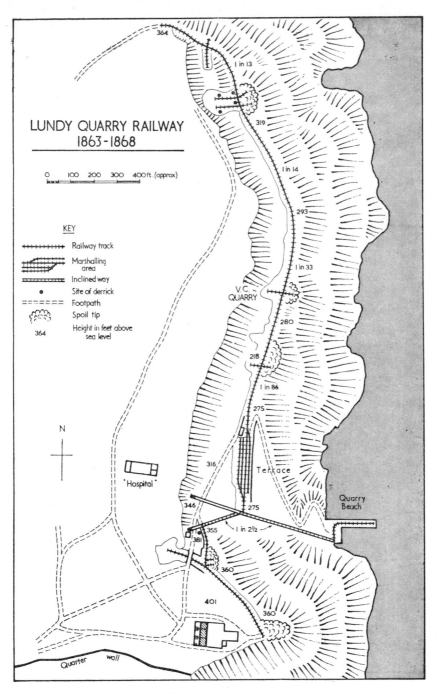

Quarry railway plan

moved to stone buildings constructed just north of Quarter Wall. The foundations of the houses still remain *in situ*. A 'hospital' and officers' block are still standing, although they are now in a ruined condition. Footpaths from these dwellings lead to a point at the south of the southernmost quarry (see map). From here a bridge, which has now vanished, but which was marked on the OS map of 1884, led to the small levelled site of the timecheck office. From here, the workmen passed northwards down the steep path to the terrace and then on to the quarries.

The actual quarries contain two levels of workings. The southernmost quarry, which is about 360 ft above sea level, is 80 ft higher than the nearest main quarry. The main quarries range from 345 ft for the small cut at the end of the northern termination of the quarry path, 319 ft for the large northern quarry, 283 ft VC quarry, 278 ft for the big quarry just south of it, and finally the terrace, which is 275 ft above sea level. The significance of this carefully graded slope will be discussed later.

There are two large earthworks in the quarry area—the largest is the terrace, which seems to have been carefully built, is level, and has traces of two buildings on it. The second was built for the timecheck office, and is equally well built and carefully battered for strength. There are also traces of straight paths.

The tramway can be traced quite clearly in dry weather from the grooves in the railbed left by the sleepers. These grooves are roughly 3 ft apart, and the sleepers seem to have been about 4 ft 3 in long, with a rail gauge of 17 in. The railbed was made up between sleepers to provide smooth going for horses. Starting at the northern end of the quarry path (see map), the tramway was built up to provide a continuous falling gradient, and from the remains of the sleeper beds it is clear that the tramway extended to a point on the plateau some 364 ft above the sea. This terminus could have been used as a loading site for heavy materials brought over the island from the landing beach, or as a changing place for the horses.

From this point the track descended to the small north quarry.

A tramway running into the quarry crosses the main line at right angles and runs towards the sea, where spoil heaps of chippings have accumulated from waste thrown over the cliff. Where these lines cross the main track there was probably a wagon turntable. The main line continues down to the big north quarry, which has two lines of track running into it, and crossing the line to end in spoil heaps on the shore. In the quarry, the lines pass four mounds, which seem to have been the bases of derricks used to load the stone on the trucks.

The main line continues to descend past VC quarry, which has one line across, to the lowest quarry, which has one spoil heap and traces of only one tramway, although there were probably two at one time. The line then reaches the terrace, where it spreads out to four parallel tracks. This was the marshalling area for the loaded trains.

The southernmost quarry seems to have been the first quarry to be opened, for it is at a higher level than all the others. Spoil was removed by a single line, which emptied over the edge of the cliff where there are traces of two small spur lines. These seem to have been abandoned early, for there was some risk that the chippings might fall down to Quarry Beach. To obviate this risk, the line was extended southwards to a point just below the officers' building on a promontory north of Quarter Wall. The worked stone was carried northwards on an almost level track which ended underneath the timecheck platform.

The worked stone from the whole quarry complex was lowered down inclines to Quarry Beach. The highest of these inclines ran from the north edge of the timecheck platform, where it was adjacent to the line from the southernmost quarry, and fell on a gradient of 1 in $2\frac{1}{2}$ to the southern end of the terrace, where it met the end of the main line from the northern quarries. From this point a longer, steeper incline led down to the beach, with a fall of 1 in $1\frac{1}{2}$. It is not clear whether the quarry tubs were themselves run down the incline, or if the stone was transferred to sliding, wheel-less containers. Progress down the incline was presumably controlled by a cable running over a pulley and counterbalanced by either a descending weight, or empty wagons being drawn up. There are no traces of an engine or winding-house at the heads of the inclines. A derrick once stood on the timecheck platform, presumably to transfer stone to the incline.

When it arrived at the beach, the stone was carried on a horizontal tramway to the jetty, and from there taken out along a wooden pier to the waiting ships. The granite company owned a steam tug, the *Vanderbyl*, which plied regularly between Lundy and Fremington Quay, where the granite was despatched by rail inland.[1]

After the liquidation of the Lundy Granite Company, a period of inactivity set in until the attempted formation of Lundy Granite Quarries in 1897 This company was to have taken over the quarries, and to have leased them for twenty-one years, paying royalties on the stone shipped out. A total of 30,000 £1 shares were issued, but only seven were taken up, and the company went into liquidation in 1900.

The seven shareholders who had subscribed to the Lundy Granite Quarries formed The Lundy & Mainland Quarries Ltd, with the object of achieving the programme set out for the previous company. In 1902, the name was changed to Lundy Island Granite Quarries Ltd, and it was decided that a royalty of 4d per ton should be paid. By 1905, 4,013 £1 shares had been taken, but nothing very much seems to have been done, and in 1909 the directors reported that their efforts had been unavailling, the lease was cancelled, and the company wound up in 1911. This marked the end of the projects for developing a granite industry on Lundy.

The possibilities opened up by the granite companies on Lundy led to the formation of the Lundy Island Floating Breakwater Company Ltd, which was registered in December 1863. The intention was to establish a floating breakwater within the roadstead on East Side, to provide for its maintenance, and also the services of a steam tug to assist vessels entering and leaving. Capital was to have been £2,000, raised in 400 shares of £5 each and a return was to have been obtained from tolls levied on vessels using the harbour. Among the list of subscribers was a Captain Christopher Claxton, of 11 Park Villas, Brompton, London SW, to whom all official notices were to be sent, but all correspondence was returned 'Not known at this address' and, in the absence of any returns, the company was dissolved by the Registrar of Joint Stock Companies in 1882.

In 1884, The Lundy Cable Company was formed to lay telegraph cables to the mainland, and to establish a signal station on the island. One thousand shares of £10 each were issued, and an agreement entered into with Lloyd's, which provided that Lloyd's should erect all the signal stations, defray working expenses, and pay the company a royalty of 2s for each message to owners and others, and an annual subsidy for duplication of such messages to the London office. It was estimated that some 80,000 vessels passed Lundy each year, and if only one-tenth of these took advantage of the company's services, an income of £880 would result. A licence to operate the telegraph was obtained from the Board of Trade, and Rogers, a London telegraph engineer, contracted to lay the ten miles of underwater cable, while a Swansea firm agreed to connect the underwater cable at Hartland Point to the inland post office. Despite the promising figures, difficulties experienced with the maintainance of the underwater cable caused the venture to be unprofitable, and the company went into liquidation in 1887.

The establishment of the air service to Lundy from Barnstaple in 1934 led to the formation of a public company in 1937, with a share capital of £10,000 in £1 shares. A mortgage of £1,000 was raised and the company bought a Short 'Scion', a 'Monospar' and a DH 60 'Moth' from Mr F. J. Perrin, who agreed to serve as manager, pilot and instructor for the company. Although a total of 4,358 shares were taken up, the company made a small loss during its first two years of operations. On the outbreak of war, the company changed its name to Atlantic Coast Airlines Ltd and leased the airfield to the Air Ministry. The balance sheet for 1944 showed a profit and the company continued in existence until 1947, when it ceased operations and was finally wound up in 1953. In 1950, Devon Air Travel resumed flights to Lundy using a De Havilland 'Rapide' twin-engined biplane. In 1952 a new company, Devonair Ltd, continued to provide air services until 1955, when the Auster aircraft used for the crossing came down in the sea and was lost. Thereafter transport to and from the island was taken over by the motor vessel *Lundy Gannet* which is owned by the Gannet Fishing Company. Although advantage has been taken of the fishing around Lundy at most times in the past, no industry has been developed and attempts in the nineteenth century to lay oyster beds were a failure.

Although not strictly an industry, the Lundy golf course was an attempt to bring visitors to the island and to encourage the tourist trade, and so merits a place in this chapter. In 1926, Major Lionel Sulivan visited Lundy on a day trip and was struck by the possibilities of a course on the island. Mr Harman became interested, and a site was chosen for a nine-hole course on Ackland's Moor, on the western side of the plateau immediately north of the Old Light. Major Sulivan agreed to lay out the course, which was opened in 1927. Campbells ran a special steamer to the opening, and the course was inaugurated by a foursome of two professionals and two amateurs. The Lundy golf club was then formed, with the services of a full-time greenkeeper/professional, but the membership apparently never exceeded twelve. The greens were kept in order until the end of the 1928 season, when the course was abandoned.

The course necessitated the construction of nine tees, nine greens and a clubhouse. A great deal of levelling was necessary for the greens, which were planted with fine turf taken from the Lighthouse field. The clubhouse was built against the west wall of the Old Light. A map and some details of the course are given Appendix F.

Among Lundy's most valuable natural assets are its simple beauty and tranquillity, together with the interest which attaches to its unusual and interesting status. Although organised day-trippers had occasionally visited Lundy since 1827 and the hotel has received guests since the late nineteenth century, it has not been until more recent times that provision for visitors has presented any considerable form of income. Visitors can now stay either at the hotel, rent one of the six holiday cottages, hire the Old Light building, or camp. In addition to such visitors, who sometimes increase the population to as many as 100 at the height of the season, the pleasure steamers call two or three times a week between Whitsun and September and each time bring several hundred visitors who spend about two hours ashore, and for whom light refreshments and souvenirs are available. All this is fortunately done without in the least distracting from the inherent qualities of the island, while helping to sustain it financially.

T HE cemetery on Beacon Hill contains the outline walls of an ancient chapel about which little is known. The St Elen to whom it is thought to have been dedicated may have been the Elen, wife of Maxim Wledig, a king of Britain who was killed in 388 AD. If the date of the original foundation is related to that of the inscribed stones which have been found nearby, then this may indeed be so.

The absence here of any known medieval burials, such as those found in Bull's Paradise, would lead to the conclusion that the Beacon Hill chapel had by that time been abandoned; and that the earliest reference, in the Rolls of 1244, to the Church of St Elena relates to a second foundation in or near Bull's Paradise itself. There is a reference in the Rolls of 1254 to a royal grant made of the living of the church of St Mary to Adam de Aston, but since this is the sole mention of a dedication to St Mary, it is more than probable that this was an error.

Lundy appears to have been regarded as a distinct parish, and the gift of the living, or advowson, was in the possession of the owner, who at this time was the king. Between the years 1325 and 1355, six rectors were presented to the living, the frequent changes possibly being due to the Black Death.

References to the incumbents are rather scanty, but there is some evidence that the rectorship of Lundy was continued until the Reformation, as upon the dissolution of the monasteries Cleeve Abbey was found to hold the 'lease' of the rectory of the island of Lundy, valued this year (1535) as worth 10s annually.

The second church, in its turn, was destroyed or fell into disrepair; archaeological evidence suggests it was abandoned early in the seventeenth century. This date accords with the written evidence of Risdon, writing at the end of the sixteenth century, who describes the remains of the chapel as still being visible. The

Page 107 : *(above)* Loading the aeroplane, 1954; *(below)* MV *Lerina*

Page 108: (above) Cattle grazing; the Old Light is in the background; (below) Operation Beef: the shipment of cattle from Lundy by landing craft in 1951

root cause of this neglect was certainly the dissolution, but the pirate occupation of Lundy is likely to have aggravated the decay.

When Bushell held Lundy around 1640, the island entered a period of continuous habitation, and the community would have required a place in which to worship. The persistent use of the name St Anne for the Lundy church in all maps dating from 1765 to 1830, together with an observation that the cement of the Beacon Hill chapel and the castle show a peculiar similarity, suggests that Bushell was responsible for both.[1] The mention by Samuel Lewis in 1831 of St Anne's and St Elena's as if they were quite distinct supports the theory that there were two chapels.

St Anne's chapel on Beacon Hill continued to be used for marriages and for occasional services until the reign of William and Mary. A description of the Beacon Hill site in 1787, however, states that '. . . an old Chapel, dedicated to St Helen . . . some of the walls remained; the entrance, built of moorstone or spar, was from the north; its length about 25 ft, breadth 12 ft, doorway 4 ft, thickness of the walls nearly $2\frac{1}{2}$ ft.' The finding of a grave below the west window of the chapel is also mentioned, as well as the burial ground that surrounded the building. This demonstrates that the building was already in a ruined condition, and unfortunately the Ordnance Survey team, which occupied the site about 1818, completed the decay by using stone from the chapel to build a cairn. The outlines of the building are all that remain today.

In 1864, the Rev Hudson Grosett Heaven, elder son of the then owner of Lundy, was licensed as curate in charge of the island, and from this time on he held two services every Sunday. At first these were held in an iron hut built by the granite company on a site in High Street, which is now used as a sheep dip; and when this building was removed, services were transferred to a large room in the farmhouse—now divided into rooms 11 and 12 of the present hotel. When he succeeded as owner, the Rev Heaven conducted services in the hall at Millcombe House, while planning to build a permanent church. Funds were insufficient to build a stone church, but Mrs Langworthy (*née* Sarah Heaven) and her sisters came forward with donations to enable a corrugated-iron church, with a spire, to be built at the top of Millcombe Valley, near the wall of the hotel garden. The church was dedicated in 1885 by Bishop Bickersteth, who described it as 'corrugated irony', but the Rev Mr Heaven was disappointed that it could only be dedicated and not consecrated, as it might in future be pulled down or used for other purposes.

A flag was flown from the flagstaff of the castle to advise crews of ships sheltering in the bay that a service was about to be held. The iron building was eventually demolished, although the foundations were left *in situ*, and used in 1955 as the foundations of a greenhouse.

A legacy from Mrs Langworthy enabled Heaven to achieve his lifetime's ambition to build a permanent stone church on the island, and in 1895 he invited tenders for the building. Britton & Pickett of Ilfracombe were awarded the contract, and their progress was rapid. The foundations were laid in the same year, and the building was completed in 1896, much of the granite being taken from the ruined Quarter Wall cottages. The contractors used their own sailing vessel, the *Kate*, to carry further building materials from Ilfracombe. The church was dedicated to St Helena, and was consecrated in 1897 by Bishop Bickersteth on a return visit to Lundy. The crossing from the mainland in the pleasure steamer *Brighton* was an unusually bad one, and the bishop, who was evidently something of a wit, acknowledged his conversion to a belief in purgatory by his experience of what it was necessary to go through in order to reach the 'kingdom of Heaven'.

The church is an example of Victorian Gothic Revival, with nave, chancel, a square tower, chiming clock and a peal of eight bells. The roof is covered by stone tiles from Tetbury, Glos, which are encrusted by myriads of small, beautifully shaped and coloured fossilised seashells. The nave has red-brick walls with a pattern of blue and cream coloured bricks inside, and a font stands by the door. In the west wall there is a large rose window, which was given by the James Heaven family, and of the two other stained glass windows, one commemorates William Hudson Heaven and his wife, and the other was designed, painted and given by an old friend of the Heavens, the Rev H. Fleming St John.

In 1905, a party of change ringers visited the church to ring a peal of Stedman Triples. After a rough crossing, the party found on landing that the bearings of the bells had suffered from the effects of the sea air. After some attention had been given to them, an attempt was made to peal the bells, but had to be abandoned. A gale developed and the party was stranded on Lundy overnight, but in the morning, after further attention had been given to the bearings, the team was able to ring a complete change before leaving the island. A plaque in the porch commemorates this feat.

A further plaque in the porch was subscribed for by members of the Heaven family, and the words on it were chosen by Marion C. H. Heaven:

> In loving memory of Hudson Grosett Heaven, Priest, Lord of the Manor of Lundy, who died in 1916 having accomplished the dream of his life by erecting this church to the Glory of God.

Possession of the advowson of Lundy has always been rather obscure. The patronage of the island church was vested in Cleeve Abbey up to the time of the dissolution, but whether it then passed with the lands of the abbey into the hands of the Yelverton family, or whether, as is more likely, it reverted to the owner of the island, is not known for a certainty. Mr W. H. Heaven assumed that the lord of the manor had the advowson right, and after his time and that of his son, the church passed to the care of the vicar of Appledore, who is appointed by the Bishop of Exeter.

Enough land was granted with the church for the building of a vicarage, but this has not yet been undertaken. In the absence of a vicarage, the present incumbent of Appledore has converted the vestry into living accommodation for his visits to the island, and occasional services are still held.

THE legal status of Lundy has long been ill-defined. The difficulties of enforcing law and order in such an isolated and outlying portion of the realm became apparent as long ago as the period of the Viking incursions, and was later shown in still stronger relief by the independence of the de Marisco family, and by the activities of the pirate settlers. Gradually, it became taken for granted that the owner of the island exercised an autonomous authority, condoned by a mainland that was practically powerless to interfere.

Mr Heaven was a jealous guardian of the rights attaching to Lundy, and made sure of their preservation by the personal maintenance of order on the island. On more than one occasion, he confiscated guns which had been brought on to the island without his permission, and refused landing permission to parties of noisy excursionists visiting in steamboats.

The rights of the owner have been called in question several times on the occasions of disputes on the island. One such case occurred at the end of 1865, probably caused by employees of the failing granite company running up bills on the mainland and then refusing or being unable to pay them. A statement at Bideford county court said 'Lundy Island was characterised as a refuge for the destitute, and some of the islanders as the fag ends of society, they being opposed to paying their debts and objecting to the presence of county court bailiffs and police constables on the island.' This resulted in an indignation meeting being held on the island, at which the name of the Bideford bailiff was freely blackened and the ancient rights of the Lundyites fully vindicated. Their bottled wrath, however, evaporated before the close of the meeting for, thinking no doubt that discretion was the better part of valour, the men resolved on a compromise, the granite company allowing the bailiffs to go in their vessel and land by making

112

their own charge. This seems only fair. The end of this matter came the following year, when a statement was given to the court that the 'Governor of the Island' would not allow any person to remain there who would not pay his debts, and that instalments would in future be paid through him.

In 1871, a man was shot dead on the island when two sailors who had come ashore became very drunk. In the small hours, they caused uproar by damaging island property and threatening anyone who tried to remonstrate with them. A posse of islanders was called out to deal with them, and a scuffle ensued. One of the islanders was carrying a shotgun, and one of the sailors, in attempting to wrest it from him, discharged it into his own chest. The following day, two policemen came with a warrant to arrest the islander, and returned to the mainland with him, together with witnesses to the struggle. He was later acquitted, and a verdict of accidental death recorded.

There was a further, rather melodramatic gun incident during the ownership of the Rev Mr Heaven, when two pilots from Bristol determined to fight a duel to the death on the island. They had got as far as wounding each other at their first confrontation when the Rev Mr Heaven got wind of the matter and promptly had them put off the island.

In spite of Lundy being extra-parochial, the inhabitants are entitled to vote at elections. In 1885, they had to poll at Woolfardisworthy, a mainland parish some miles inland, but as a result of the Representation of The Peoples Act of 1918, a polling booth was erected on the island for the general election in that year, the first and only time such a thing has been done. In 1921 there were eight electors and in the 1922 election there were thirteen, of whom eight recorded their vote at Instow. In January 1924 the *Lerina* carried fourteen islanders to vote at Instow. In 1950 the Boundary Commission declared Lundy to be in the constituency of Torrington.

An interesting court case arose in 1931 out of a decision by Mr Harman to issue his own coins for use on the island. The following is an extract from *The Times* report :[1]

The appellant, Mr Martin Coles Harman, who is the owner of the fee simple of Lundy Island, was charged on April 15th, 1930, on an information preferred by the respondent, Police Superintendant William Bolt, that on a date unknown, between November 14th, 1929 and March 5th, 1930, he unlawfully issued as a token for money a piece of metal to the value of one halfpenny, contrary to Section 5 of the Coinage Act 1870. The Justices convicted Mr Harman and fined him £5 and 15 gns costs. The following facts were proved or admitted : the applicant was the owner in fee simple of Lundy Island, which is situated some 12 miles from the coast of Devon, and some 28½ miles from the Welsh coast. No rates, taxes or duties of customs and excise had in fact been levied or collected by the Crown or Imperial Parliament in the Island of Lundy. The High Court of Justice had exercised Jurisdiction over the island in that in the year 1321 the Justices Itinerant in Devonshire, heard and determined a dispute relating to the ownership thereof. There was no evidence before the Justices of any subsequent fact ousting the Jurisdiction. On one occasion—in 1925—a Coroner's Inquest was held on the island, when the Coroner for North Devon held an Inquest on a body found drowned off the coast of the island. The appellant's predecessor in title entered a protest against the holding of that inquest by the Crown, but the inquest was nevertheless held.

On December 18th 1871, one Charles Treleven was arrested on the island by a Police Constable of the Devon Constabulary under a warrent signed by a Justice of the Peace for the County of Devon, and was brought before the Devon Magistrates on a charge of Murder. The appellant's predecessor in title, Mr William Hudson Heaven, protested against the execution of that warrant on the island. In 1897 two men were charged before the Devon Justices on a charge of stealing copper from a wreck on Lundy Island, and one of them was committed for trial to the Devon Quarter Sessions. Four inhabitants of the island, including the appellant, were on the register of Parliamentary Electors for the polling district of Instow, in the County of Devon. The Justices had before them correspondence which passed in 1871 between the Home Secretary, the Chief Constable of Devon, and Mr Heaven. The appellant also put in, in evidence, an agreement dated November 25th, 1929, between himself, the Board of Trade, and the Corporation of Trinity House relating to the establishment of a look-out on Lundy Island. A copy of the latest edition of the official Lists of Courts of Summary Jurisdiction published by the Home Office in 1913 was put in in evidence. Applications for the old-age pensions by persons resident on Lundy Island had been entertained by the authorities for the County of Devon. On November 19th 1918 the Justices for the County of Devon had appointed a special constable for the island.

On June 6th, 1929, the appellant gave an order to the Mint, Birmingham, Ltd, for 50,000 bronze tokens about the size of a penny, and a similar quantity about the size of a halfpenny, and these tokens were delivered to the appellant who, between November 14th 1929, and March 5th 1930, issued them on Lundy Island as tokens for money. They were not issued by or with the approval of His Majesty's Royal Mint. The appellant contended that : Lundy Island was situated outside the territorial waters of the United Kingdom and was not within the body of the County of Devon, but was outside the realm for all practical purposes, and that he had the right to exercise such rights as he thought fit on the island, that the Justices had no jurisdiction, and that the information was misconceived. Apart from raising these contentions, the appellant refused to plead to the information, and took no part in the proceedings before the justices.

The respondent contended that the Court had jurisdiction and that the offence had been proved. The Justices were of the opinion that they had jurisdiction. They found the charge proved and convicted the appellant. The question of law for the Court was whether their determination that they had jurisdiction was correct. Mr Harman appeared in person. The Attorney General (Sir William Jowett KC) and Mr Wilfred Lewis, appeared for the respondent. Mr Harman said it was quite true that he had issued on Lundy Island coins called Puffins and Half Puffins. The Puffin was a bird very common on Lundy Island, the very name of which was Puffin Island, *Lunde* being Icelandic for puffin. The Lundians usually referred to the mainland as the 'adjacent island'. The importance of Lundy Island was not to be gauged by its mere size or population. Its services to navigation had been enormous. So long as it was responsibly well governed, the mainland had not interfered but the mainland authorities repudiated all responsibility when anything really called for intervention, such as the murder of the entire population.

Lord Chief Justice: Does that often happen? (laughter)
Mr Harman: It has happened two or three times in the past.
Mr Justice Avery: The population of what? Rabbits?
Mr Harman: There are about a thousand rabbits to every human

115

being, but the residents number about forty-five apart from visitors. Lundy pays no rates, taxes, or custom duties, and that is right because it received nothing from the mainland. I claim that Lundy Island is a vest-pocket-size self-governing dominion. We are all loyal subjects of the British Empire, and desired that this case be referred to King George for His Majesty's decision.

Turning to the findings in the case, Mr Harman said that the case in the fourteenth century could not be relied on by the Crown, whether it was referred voluntarily to the Judges to decide a matter which could not be decided on the island, or whether the Judges dealt with it in the normal course, for the decision was that they could not give a judgement which could not be enforced on the island. As to the statement that four persons, including himself were on the Parliamentary Register, the Conservative agent was invited over for a game of cricket (laughter) and went home and got the islanders put on the register. A form was sent every year, and the names of those who had died or removed were struck off, but no new names were added, and the numbers of electors was diminishing.

Mr Justice MacKinnon: If I addressed a letter to you at your house on Lundy Island who would deliver it?

Mr Harman: I should.

Mr Justice MacKinnon: When I went over to the island once, I understood that it was the post boat which took me.

Mr Harman: That must have been some years ago.

Mr Justice MacKinnon: Yes, it was in Mr Heaven's time.

Mr Harman: I dismissed the GPO and issue my own stamps. I convey my letters bearing these stamps to Instow Post Office where they must be stamped with ordinary English stamps, and I collect at Instow the letters addressed to the island and distribute them.

It was most unfair, said Mr Harman, to cite against him the things that happened during the war, such as the appointment of a special constable, for Lundy, like other parts of the Empire, did everything required to assist the prosecution of the war, and every man who left Lundy to go to the war was killed. The police came over disguised as trippers. Why, if they were entitled to come, did they not come over in uniform and state their mission? When they last came, forty years ago, they were hustled into the sea. Who was in fact governing Lundy if it were not he and his agent?

Mr Justice Avery: Who is the sovereign of Lundy Island?

Mr Harman: I am; but the island is a self-governing Dominion of the British Empire recognising King George as its head.

The Lundians, said Mr Harman, were happy and hard-working and there was no unemployment in the island. With regard to Treleven in 1871, the case stated was inaccurate. Mr Heaven refused to allow him to be arrested on the island, but as he could not give him a fair trial on the island, he escorted Treleven to Ilfracombe and there still maintained that the police could not arrest one of his subjects, but made himself responsible for Treleven's appearance to take his trial.

The Attorney-General said that Lundy Island, from what they had heard, was a sort of Utopia. But why should the people be more happy with Puffins and Half Puffins bearing Mr Harman's head than with pence or halfpence bearing King George's head? Many modern statutes and orders recognised Lundy Island as part of the County of Devon. He referred to the County Courts Order of 1899, to the Schedule of the Representation of the Peoples Act 1918 and to the Wild Birds Protection Order, 1930 (SR & O 1930 No 957). The Territorial Waters Act, 1878, declared that Great Britain included 'adjacent islands'. This seemed to be one point which the income-tax collectors had overlooked. It might be that they would now put it right. Mr Harman, in reply, submitted that the making of Acts of Parliament and Statutory Orders relating to Lundy, without the consent of the people of Lundy, and declaring it to be part of the County of Devon, 'cut no ice' any more than an act of Lundy declaring Devonshire to be part of Lundy Island would 'cut any ice'. If the income-tax authorities sought to include Lundy Island, he might be able to recover some thousands of pounds if he could bring Lundy Island, which was run at a loss, into his general tax position.

The Lord Chief Justice, in giving judgement, said that it was a very entertaining case and had been very ably argued by the appellant. His argument was that he was the owner in fee simple of Lundy Island, that it was situate outside the territorial waters of Great Britain and was not part of the body of the County of Devon, and that the information was misconceived. That seemed to be a question of fact, and the question was whether there was evidence to entitle the Justices to come to the conclusion to which they came. He thought that there was much evidence. In particular, there were four of the inhabitants, including the appellant, on the parliamentary register. The attention of the Court had been called to a number of Statutes and Orders in which Lundy had been treated sometimes by Parliament, and sometimes by the executive, as part of the County of Devon. The able argument of the appellant was that all that had been done without the express consent of the inhabitants of Lundy, but he (his Lordship) did not think that that was an argument to which the court could listen in that case and the appeal must be dismissed. Mr Justice Avery and Mr Justice MacKinnon agreed.

Following the High Court judgement, the remaining puffin coins have been sold on Lundy as souvenirs only, although the island stamps continue to be issued in puffin values. This case seems to have struck at the roots of Lundy's autonomy as far as the administration of justice goes, but the island still manages to be an exception to the usual administrative and legislative interference suffered elsewhere, so perhaps the Attorney-General's appellation 'Utopia' may yet be true.

Shortly after the Italian attack on Ethiopia, a Finnish vessel requested permission to land on Lundy some ammunition destined for the struggle. This was, of course, refused, whereupon the ship sailed for Sark, which the captain felt was similar to Lundy and, in some indefinite way, independent of League of Nations control. Needless to say, permission was also refused there, and the cargo had eventually to be landed in Arabia.

Since the Isles of Scilly became subject to income tax in April 1953, Lundy and Sark are the only parts of the British Isles not subject to this tax. No attempt has been made to collect revenue on Lundy since the time of Sir John Borlase Warren, when a revenue officer spent seven years on the island, and collected no more than £5 in all. As recently as May 1969, Lord Antrim, Chairman of the National Trust, whose acquisition of the island had just been announced, confirmed that the island's residents would keep their tax-free haven.

Lundy's inhabitants pay no rates, there are no gun or dog licences, and the island tractors are not subject to road fund tax. This is, however, strict justice, as the inhabitants do not receive the services for which these taxes are raised on the mainland. The only levy which the islanders do pay is the National Health contribution, from which they are entitled to benefit in the same way as the population of the British Isles at large. It is still presumed that the owner holds himself responsible for order on the island, and that the police have no authority there, although the Devon County Council have sent a memorandum to the Boundaries Commission in an endeavour to find the solution to this enigma, particularly as far as crime and local government are concerned. Recently, for the purpose of agricultural subsidies, the Ministry of Agriculture have classified the island as a hill farm, so further links with the mainland are being forged.

The coinage mentioned above, which was issued on the island by Mr Harman, was not the only money to be peculiar to the island. A member of the British Numismatic Society pointed out in a lecture[2] that Bushell, who held Lundy for the Crown in the Civil Wars, probably minted coins there. He must have had his mint with him on the island, as Oxford, the site of the last royal mint, had fallen to the Parliamentary forces. The coins he issued bear the mint mark A for 1645, and B or a plume for 1646, and resemble those which were made at Bushell's Bristol mint. It has been argued that the A and B coins were struck at Appledore and Barnstaple respectively, as these towns held out for the King until 1646 and were accessible for six months after Bristol had fallen. Against this is the consideration that the privilege of coining in Devon and Cornwall had been vested in Sir Richard Vyvian, who, had he struck coins in Appledore or Barnstaple, would have used dies from his mint at Exeter. Lundy, being a secure fortress, would have offered the most suitable place for the operations, and as it was never blockaded, bullion and coins could have been imported and exported safely.

Mr Harman's puffins and half-puffins were minted in 1929 of the same bronze alloy as the regular coinage, and were minted for him by Ralph Heaton & Sons of Birmingham. On the obverse of the coins is a profile of Mr Harman and the words 'Martin Coles Harman 1929', while the reverse has a puffin bird and 'Lundy One Puffin' or 'Lundy Half Puffin' and a profile head of the puffin. The coins are not milled, but are inscribed round the edge 'Lundy Lights and Leads'. The coins were current only on Lundy, where the normal English coinage was used concurrently. Harman arranged with the Bideford banks to exchange English copper for Lundy coins, and this arrangement continued until the High Court ruling of 1931. In 1965, the dies were taken over by a firm known as Modern World Coins, who issued a double commemorative set of coins on the fortieth anniversary of the purchase of Lundy by Mr Harman.

Another distinction possessed by Lundy and quickly noticed by visitors is its exemption from the mainland licensing laws, and the Marisco tavern is open to all at such hours as are dictated by demand.

11   THE ARCHAEOLOGY OF LUNDY

BY K. S. GARDNER

ARCHAEOLOGY today is more than just another name for Prehistory; more than just tombs and temples, it is a study of man's past struggles to come to terms with his environment, to live in the broadest sense off the land. Logically, in this broad view, the nineteenth-century engineer and the first neolithic farmer are of equal importance and equal interest. Since the mid-1950s, it has been the writer's privilege to direct reseach into the rich field of Lundy's archaology, under the aegis of the Lundy Field Society, and it has been the policy to seek to trace the profile of the total archaeology of the 1,000 acres of granite.

Two factors greatly aided the task :

(i) Lundy, as an island, is a clearly defined geographical unit on which the varying patterns of land use can be studied without confusion with adjacent estates.

(ii) The historical research which forms the basis of much of this book has also provided a most useful base for the study of medieval and post-medieval archaeology.

Pleistocene

During the glacial fluctuations of the Ice Ages, Lundy was alternately a sea-girt isle and a rocky tor at the mouth of the Severn estuary. Research has recently indicated that the Pen-Ultimate Glaciation actually encroached on to Lundy's plateau, depositing moraine and grinding down the top of coastal crags. The comparatively large valley systems, such as Gannet's Combe and Millcombe, were possibly formed by drainage of melt-water at this stage. The eventual rise of interglacial sea level left 'raised beach' phenomena, particularly near Brazen Ward, which were themselves subsequently overburdened with Ultimate Peri-Glacial

121

'Mead'. No trace of man's activity has yet been found associated with these early features.

Mesolithic

Following the last recession of the Polar Front, there was an improvement in climate, and a consequent change in flora and fauna. This was reflected by a change in man's equipment, and there evolved a series of cultures typical of the Mesolithic period. Marked by small flint points and barbs for setting in wooden hafts, and with distinctive waste products, this culture arrived in post-glacial Britain some 8000 BC, before separation from the Continent and probably before Lundy's last separation from Devon.

THE BRICK FIELDS

The first indication of man's presence on Lundy is an assemblage of such worked flints and wasteflakes recovered from the Tillage and Brick Fields. Although poor in quality and made from local beach pebble flint, which itself was probably brought to the locality by glacial action, the collection includes crude forms of microliths, microburins and conical and bi-polar cores. It probably derives from the camping site of a nomadic group, whose economy included, if it was not entirely based upon, the fish and seabird food supply. It is not reasonable to ascribe a date to this collection—the poor quality product is perhaps due as much to the nature of the basic raw material as to the lack of skill in the artificer. It could represent a late survival into subsequent Neolithic times, which would have involved the group in a marine crossing, but if it actually is the remains of a pure Mesolithic hunting group, it could date from pre-7000 BC, by which time the Bideford Bay flats were being flooded by the Flandrian Marine Transgression.

Neolithic

About 3500 BC, while the nomadic hunters were still tied economically to the small game of the forests and fens, men of superior tradition arrived from the mainland of Europe. These were skilled in the working of stone, they bowed to a powerful religion, and above all, they came with the knowledge and experience of agriculture—of growing crops and controlling animals. They were advanced enough to produce distinctive pottery and organised enough to trade goods over hundreds of miles.

Lundy's hut circles and pygmy flints have sometimes been ascribed to this Neolithic period, and with the island's position on the main maritime migration route from Western Europe to Wales and the Severn—Cotswold areas, it would seem to be a suitable place of shelter and revictualling for Neolithic migrants. Having said this, however, it must be added that not one piece of material evidence has come to light to support the hypothesis of Neolithic occupation.

Bronze-Iron Age

About 2000 BC, a fresh influx of settlers came into southern England, who, among their technical attributes, included the ability to obtain, blend, and work metals. Their cultural monuments include the round burial mound, from which most of the archaeological evidence has come for the early phase of their occupation of the mainland. Occupation sites are scarce until about 1200 BC, although the subsequently undeveloped highlands of south Devon and Cornwall are still comparatively rich in the remains of farmsteads consisting of circular stone houses and small field plots. The tradition of such farmsteads continued into the succeeding Iron Age which, in the far west, tended initially to blend into a sort of Bronze Age continuum, and to develop eventually into a definitive form of Celtic culture which was to survive for a thousand years.

GANNET'S COMBE

On Lundy, traces are apparent of the pattern of farming from about 1000 BC until probably well into the Christian era. There are three main centres of settlement, although traces of huts and fields are present almost all over the island. The earliest is a settlement of late Bronze Age type, occupying the plateau north of Gannet's Combe. Here a low wall encloses a dozen stone huts, some actually contiguous with the enclosure wall, and in a good state of preservation. Some of the huts are about 10 ft in diameter and are conjoined with rectangular chambers, while others are closer to 30 ft across. One of the larger examples at the North End contained a bed bench of a type similar to huts on Dean Moor, Devon. A further group of huts lies south-east of the Combe, and there are occasional outliers as far as Threequarter Wall.

MIDDLE PARK

Judging by the existing field remains, the second main settlement lies between Threequarter Wall and Halfway Wall, where low grass banks, ploughed-out traces of Celtic field systems are associated with hut sites and possible cairn circles (or ruined burial cairns). Around Tibbett's Hill and south of Halfway Wall these field boundaries continue as unploughed stone banks, and, the remains of a large bi-cellular hut [?], probably date from the first century BC, indicated by pottery obtained from trial excavations.

SOUTH FARM

The third main area runs south from Quarter Wall, where again ploughed-over grass banks define the old fields, and circular mounds mark the sites of former huts.

Excavations at Beacon Hill and Ackland's Moor have produced pottery akin to sites in Cornwall, and dated there to the last few hundred years BC. There are, however, many problems in interpreting these sites in detail from the minimal trenching undertaken, but broadly speaking, they represent the farming occupation over the last thousand years BC which probably continued well into the Christian era.

Page 125: (above) *Carmine Filomena* aground off Rat Island, 1938; (below) *Maria Kyriakides* aground below the quarries, 1929

Page 126: (left) Shag; *(right)* Puffin

An interesting feature revealed by a study of a nineteenth-century estate map is that the Ackland's Moor Celtic field system appears to have remained as the basis for agriculture until the mid-nineteenth century.

The invasion of Britain by the Roman Emperor Claudius in 43 AD caused the old native Iron Age society to decline culturally and to be replaced, in lowland Britain at least, by a more sophisticated economy. In the highland zone, however, the influence of Rome was minimal, and in Wales and the south-west the native Celtic traditions tended to survive and eventually emerge as the basis of a Sub-Roman culture in the fifth and sixth centuries AD. On Lundy, even more remote than the highland moors, there has yet been discovered no evidence of Romanisation. A few sherds of Roman pottery in Bristol Museum may have come from the island, but the old records are confused on the point. In the literary field, both Richmond and Frere attribute the description by the Roman geographer Solinus of an island off the Devon/Cornwall coast to Lundy. They specifically claim that certain conditions and social habits prevailed on Lundy in Roman times. It would be tempting to accept their identification without question, but in fairness it must be said that the less publicised case for Solinus's island being Scilly is much more logical.

Early Christian

Following the collapse of Imperial control over Britain, the eastern lowland zone was quickly invested by Saxons, Angles and Jutes. In the comparatively remote and un-Romanised west, however, the Celtic communities had developed into a more independent form of society, in which Christianity was to seed and flower under the influence of (mainly) Irish missionaries.

On Lundy, efforts are still being made to unravel the late Celtic continuum from the more diagnostic Early Iron Age—but they have yet to succeed in finding out exactly where the islanders lived in the fifth/sixth centuries AD, although a few scraps of imported Mediterranean pottery of the period have turned up just north of the present village.

H

If it is not yet known where they lived, it is possible to be fairly certain of where they were buried, for perhaps the most significant site on the island is the Early Christian cemetery on Beacon Hill. It is a roughly oval enclosure on the western cliffs and contains many unmarked and undated grave mounds. One, a squarish flat-topped cairn, or 'leacht', is possibly the special grave of a saint—perhaps the founder of the Christian community there. There is a collection of nineteenth- and twentieth-century graves in the vicinity of a ruined chapel (probably medieval), but the most important feature is the assemblage of four Early Christian memorial stones, which alone establish Lundy high on the list of Early Christian sites in Britain. The inscriptions are :

(1) . . . IGERNI . . . I. TIGERNI	fifth/sixth century
(2) ⊕ POTITI	? eighth century
(3) OPTIMI	fifth/sixth century
(4) RESTEUTA	fifth/sixth century

How the end of Lundy's undocumented or pre-historic phase came, is unknown. With the longboats of the Norsemen scavenging the western waters, it could not have been long before the shelter of Lundy Road drew them. One visit would have been enough to plunge the community of Christian farmers into oblivion, or perhaps they discreetly abandoned their rocky home in good time.

Medieval

From the eighth–ninth centuries, when the Saxons were consolidating their holdings in the West, until the late eleventh century when the Duke of Normandy relieved them of the responsibility, the Atlantic coastline received many seaborne visitations. Of the movements about her of Norse, Dane, Irish and even presumably the Saxon royal fleet, Lundy maintains a frustrating silence. It is left to the Viking activities of an audacious freeman of Wales to lift the veil of the Dark Ages and allow the first glimmer of history to reveal the Lundy of the mid-twelfth century. The Orkneyinga Saga of AD 1148 reveals that he found an apparently impregnable stronghold on Lundy. His name is lost to us, but he could possibly have been one of the de Mariscos who certainly held the island from AD 1154, and possibly from AD 1135, and who, although of Norman stock, had strong connections with Wales.

THE STRONGHOLD

The site of the de Marisco's stronghold is to the west of the High Street rickyards in Bull's Paradise. Here, in the earliest phase, there was some sort of stone structure with a flagged floor, possibly associated with a rock-cut ditch. The few pottery fragments from this level suggest a date of at least the twelfth century, if not earlier, so this may well have been the sea rover stronghold. This particular structure was levelled and replaced by a massive granite wall 7 ft thick, which enclosed a yard containing traces of lean-to and free-standing buildings, with a hearth and clay-lined waterhole. The occupation material is sparse, the waterhole producing the best evidence of thirteenth-century usage. The site again seems to have been levelled, much of the stone from the walls being removed from the site, the rest filling the waterhole and ditches. Pottery of the late thirteenth century—early seventeenth century was contained in an extensive rubbish tip which overlay the demolition level. From this time, history and archaeology go hand-in-hand, and the pattern of thirteenth-century building and demolition revealed by the spade is reflected by the records of the realm.

The de Mariscos were a high-born and influential family, and with their estates and coastal port in Somerset to the east, and their holdings as Lord Justiciary of Ireland to the west, the island was ideally positioned to enable them to control the waters of the Bristol and St George's Channels. Their seafaring ability made one of them Admiral of the Fleet to King John, but their general lawlessness often brought them into sharp conflict with the Crown. In 1222, during one of their more popular periods, they were granted permission to strengthen the defences of Lundy by transferring to it some of their great siege-engines from Somerset.

THE MANGONEL BATTERY AND CASTLE 1

The site of one of these thirteenth-century artillery batteries has been located on a revetted granite crag high above the western landing beach on Jenny's Cove, and a few scraps of pottery from the foundations seem in keeping with the thirteenth-century wares. Pottery of indentical fabric was found in the foundations of the 7-ft thick wall in Bull's Paradise, and it may well be that this structure was also part of a programme of defensive works at this time.

The period 1222–42 saw a marked decline in the royal relations with the de Mariscos, and following their attempt on the life of Henry III the island was taken, a de Marisco executed and the keep and bailey built for the royal constable. While this castle was being constructed, the archives record that the king's buildings were repaired, but it seems a logical hypothesis that once the constable's castle was habitable, the redundant de Marisco stronghold should be demolished, as is borne out by the archaeological evidence.

CEMETERY 2

Late Medieval

There now followed a series of less turbulent tenures which lasted some 300 years. The site of the old stronghold became a levelled yard [?], but some time after 1425 the area immediately south of it was used as a Christian cemetery, with graves dug through a thin black rubbish layer which has yielded coins of early fifteenth-century date. The graves run in lines from north to south, with heads to the west, and were mostly covered with granite slabs. One slab and one re-erected headstone have been left *in situ*, and other slabs may be seen in the wall fabric of the adjacent farmbuilding. Associated with the cemetery (which has now produced over twenty skeletons) are the slight foundations of a rectangular building, also post-thirteenth century, which could have been a chapel. The whole site was desecrated and covered with a rubbish midden of food bones, limpet shells and pottery by the early seventeenth century.

GIANTS' GRAVES

Among Lundy's few previously reported archaeological sites are the so-called Giants' Graves, discovered in 1860 during farm construction work. Two skeletons, allegedly 8 ft in length, were found enclosed in a stone tomb, and seven other skeletons, buried in a row, and a mass of other human bones were found. Three glass beads 'from the Giants' Graves' are in the Bristol Museum, where they have been dated as the ninth century AD. The reconstruction by Loyd, incorporating the pillow stone (now in the church porch) lent credence to the early claim that the burials were of Viking origin. Space does not permit a full discussion here, suffice it to say that, in view of the available evidence, the Giants' Graves have not been shown to be other than contemporary with the rest of the cemetery.

(i) The beads—even if of ninth century—appear from Chanter not to have been associated with the 'giants', but with the mass of disarticulated bones. These may well have been re-interments of previously discovered graves (*qv* grave slabs in farm walls), in which case the beads lose their value as dating evidence.

(ii) The early references 1860, 1870, and 1877 give three different descriptions of the main tomb, which starts off as a hollowed stone coffin (medieval?), and finishes as a complicated cist reconstructed figuratively by Loyd in 1925.

(iii) The adjacent graves excavated in 1928 by Dr Bristowe, in 1933 by Dr Dollar and Mr T. C. Lethbridge, and those cleared in 1964, have all yielded evidence of a post-thirteenth century pre-seventeenth century cemetery. The possibility always remains, however, of a Viking grave having been used as the *raison d'être* for the later cemetery being sited away from Beacon Hill. The ecclesiastical problems raised by these two Christian cemeteries are discussed elsewhere.

WIDOW'S TENEMENT

Throughout the late medieval period we assume at present that the castle of the constable was the main dwelling place. One other building can be seen north of Threequarter Wall, set in its own farm enclosure. This, the Widow's Tenement, is a fine example of a medieval longhouse measuring 45 ft by 15 ft. At the east end is the byre where the cattle were stalled, and at the west, raised above the adjacent floor level, was the farmer's living area. The north and south walls have the traditional opposite doors, there is a cross wall to restrain cattle, and possibly a cattle door leading from an adjacent walled enclosure or yard. The living end, or solar, has a narrow entrance at the north-west, and what appears to be an oven or kiln. Two other enclosed yards abutt to the north and to the south-west. The main enclosure of seventeen acres in which the house is set also includes an earlier Iron Age[?] hut and a quarry with unfinished circular millstones.

BRAZEN WARD AND NORTH END

Post-Medieval

A general lack of constructive activity on Lundy during the later medieval and early post-medieval periods is reflected both in the archives and in the field. The island was nominally held by gentlemen of repute, but in fact was often unoccupied except on a temporary basis by pirates of various nationalities and creeds. Presumably, their tenures were destructive, or at least permissive of natural decay as far as the structures of farm and church were concerned. Elizabeth's war with Spain suggests a new concern for Lundy's anchorage, and the documentary evidence supports this, as Grenville was warned to fortify it. The Civil War saw a great deal of Royalist money spent on fortification, and in 1787 a reference is made to over forty old platforms on which guns were placed in 'Queen Anne's war with the French'. Of these forty, less than a quarter have so far been located, mostly around the north-east coast. Most impressive of these is the Brazen Ward, controlling a natural landing-place on the east side. A heavily constructed breastwork protects a promenade between gun platforms and a square, cellar-like building with a 6-ft thick wall—possibly the powder store. Pottery suggests a Tudor date, although tradition maintains that it was constructed by Lord Saye and Sele after the Civil War.

Looking north across the cove from Brazen Ward, another revetted gun platform can be seen, and a further series exists between Gannet's Rock and the North Light. The first of these is a revetted platform 250 yd north of Gannet's Rock, with a second on the north-east point of the island, and 60 yd west of this, at the same level, is a building with a fireplace and stone seat—possibly the garrison quarters. Above these and just below plateau level, is a small square foundation overlooking the north-east quarter, and on the plateau is the ruined John O'Groat's cottage. This was apparently occupied by fowlers in the early nineteenth century, but could have served as a military watchpost. It, too, has a fireplace and stone bench.

CASTLE 2

The castle keep shows signs of much post-medieval alteration, including nineteenth-century cottages inserted into its shell. The 'sham' embrasures, however, appear in the 1775 engraving by Grosse, and could conceivably be part of the Royalist Governor Bushell's repair work. The castle parade is a good example of a seventeenth-century gun battery with a diamond-shaped gun-port to the east commanding the landing bay. Another has collapsed to the south. Below the parade to the east is a man-made subterranean chamber with a masonry lined, and possibly once roofed, forecourt. It is known as Benson's Cave after the smuggling Bideford merchant, who, it is claimed, used it as a store for his contraband. The 1775 engraving shows a capstan in front of the cave, apparently used for hauling items from the beach below. Dated mural graffiti suggest that the cave was in use before Benson's day, and it may in fact date from the Civil War. Governor Bushell is thought to have withdrawn his royal mint to Lundy, and such a cavern within the castle bailey would have been an ideal strongroom, and well within Bushell's constructional abilities as a mining engineer.

The late eighteenth century saw the building of the present farmhouse, but to judge from the early nineteenth-century maps, the fields in use were still basically the same old plots laid out over 2,000 years previously. With the mid-nineteenth century development under the Heavens' ownership, the present farm layout and much of the present village appeared. A short-lived attempt commercially to quarry and export the granite gave Lundy its latest archaeological feature—a ruined industrial settlement with railway, jetty, administration and accommodation buildings, some of which, north of Quarter Wall, were stripped to their foundations to provide stone for the church in 1890. Lundy, for all its wealth of history and archaeology, has changed but little at the hand of man. Therein, perhaps, lies its greatest charm.

REFERENCES

CHAPTER ONE

1 Mrs M. C. H. Heaven.
2 Mr M. C. Harman bought Grassholm for his elder son, John, but sold it back to the original owner after John Harman died.
3 Journal of 1787. Entry dated 10.7.1781. This journey was almost certainly made along the East Side path, as the West Side path does not appear even on Chanter's map of 1877 and probably did not come into use until the erection of the telegraph poles in 1910.
4 One theory is that they were sold to a salvage company and raised from the sea bed; another that they were taken to Cardiff Castle, but this has been refuted by the late Marquis of Bute. Yet another theory is that they were salvaged by a tenant farmer and sold to Mr F. R. Crawshay about 1865 and mounted by him on his yacht *Querida*.
5 Mrs M. C. H. Heaven : 'So-called by the Heaven family; misnamed Long Ruse on OS map'.
6 The descriptive 'Devil's' is used throughout the country in naming natural features of unusual proportion.
7 *North Devon Magazine*, 1824, p 57, quoting journal of 1787.
8 *Home Friend*, 1853, vol 3, no 54. The name may derive from the 'rattling' noise made by the granite boulders caught in the swell on the sea bed in this bay.

CHAPTER TWO

1 Mrs M. C. H. Heaven.
2 *Life of Edward II*, p 599.
3 Chancery Proceedings 1776.
4 *Home Friend*, 1853, vol 3, no 57, p 98.

CHAPTER THREE

1 Lundy Field Society's Annual Report, 1954.
2 H. R. Smith : *Saxon England*, 1953, pp 576–7.
3 R. Deacon : *Madoc and the Discovery of America*, 1967, p 41.

135

4 William, son of Jordan, inherited Lundy on the death of his father in 1234. *Calendar of Inquisitions and Postmortems.*

5 John Lawrence : *A History of Capital Punishment,* p 6 : 'Hanging, drawing and quartering was invented for the express benefit of a William Maurice, the son of a nobleman, who was convicted not of treason but of piracy'.

6 Heraldic evidence supports this as the arms of the de Marisco family were 'Gules a lion rampant argent' and that of William de Marisco (d 1242) were 'Or a lion rampant sable langues gules'. See *Coll. Top. et Gen.,* vol 4, p 75. A lion rampant suggests high nobility, if not royalty.

7 Stephen (son of Herbert) de Marisco died in 1374 without issue.

8 *Calendar of State Papers, Foreign Series,* no 668, 12.5.1559.

9 Ibid, no 693, 16.5.1559.

CHAPTER FOUR

1 Lord Bath in *Petitionary Remonstrance* says that Bushell 'rebuilt the castle from the ground', and Meyrick in *History of the County of Cardigan,* (introduction : p 219) that Bushell 'constructed a harbour at Lundy where his vessels might lie in safety'.

2 Newcastle, 14.7.1646.

3 Lord Saye and Sele offered to sell the island to Bushell for £3,000 at this time but, being already in debt, Bushell's main interest in remaining on Lundy lay in its use as a bargaining counter for favourable terms for surrender.

4 The garrison was twenty-one men, including Bushell.

5 *North Devon Magazine,* 1824, vol 1, pp 51–62, quoting journal of 1787.

6 'He planted there a small Irish colony, and drew up for them a compendious code, including a quaint law of divorce in case of matrimonial disputes'. Undated newspaper cutting inside a copy of *Chanter* in the North Devon Athenaeum.

CHAPTER SIX

1 Hartland Chronicle, 15.6.1919.

CHAPTER SEVEN

1 *North Devon Journal,* 25.1.1866.

2 Ibid, 21.12.1882.

REFERENCES

CHAPTER EIGHT

1 The belief that Lundy granite was used in building the Thames Embankment is erroneous, and was so established by the late Mr A. E. Blackwell in correspondence with the London County Council surveyor's office.

CHAPTER NINE

1 *Chanter*, p 99. Analysis carried out in 1965 by the Building Research Station tends to disprove this, but Chanter may have had access to indisputably original samples of cement.

CHAPTER TEN

1 *The Times*, 14.1.1931.
2 *British Numismatic Journal*, 1927–8, vol 19.

CHAPTER ELEVEN

Prof I. A. Richmond : *Roman and Native in North Britain*, p. 118; Prof F. Freerer : *Britannia* p 371.

Chronological Table of Sites and Gazetteer

Period	Type of Site	Location	National Grid Reference	Remarks
Mesolithic	Flint-working area	Fields E of airfield	SS 137-447-	Flints found when fields ploughed
Bronze Age	Hut compound	From Gannet's Combe to North End	13304780	Stone compound wall with contiguous double huts; single huts to N
Iron Age	Hut sites and field plots	SE of Gannet's Combe	13604710	Hut sites
		S of Halfway Wall to Ponds-bury	13724573	Stone field walls; bicellular hut E of east track
		Between Halfway and Three-quarter Walls	13644598	Grass-covered field banks in centre of island and E of east track
			13864632	Stone walls on Tibbett's Hill with hut sites
			13534625	? Two huts/cairn circles in central pasture-land
		Ackland's Moor	13184473	S of Quarter Wall; stone circles and alignments (huts and plots)
				Grass-covered field bank N of Old Light
		Beacon Hill	13224421	Huts of Old Light with contiguous field bank superimposed by Christian cemetery; field banks cover S end of island
	'Kistvaen'	S end of wall running S from Old Light	13624371	Hollow in ground; ? capstone in adjacent field

Period	Type of site	Location	National Grid Reference	Remarks
Dark Age	Pottery find	Field SE of airfield	13754445	Imported Mediterranean hard red ware found in ploughing
	Cemetery	Beacon Hill	13254427	Early Christian memorial stones platform cairn
Medieval	Structural foundations	Bull's Paradise, W of High Street	13654422	Foundations with ? twelfth-century pottery
	Stronghold	Bull's Paradise, W of High Street	13654422	Enclosure wall 7 ft thick, buildings and well in yard, thirteenth century
	Mangonel battery	N of W end Halfway Wall	13334586	Revetted platform above Jenny's Cove; walls at lower levels
	Keep and bailey	S end	14144377	Ruined keep and bailey bank and internal ditch 1242 AD
	Longhouse and enclosure	N of Threequarter Wall	13584686	Widow's Tenement, thirteenth/fourteenth century
	Cemetery and ? chapel	Bull's Paradise field	13654418	Christian cemetery, grave slabs and rectangular building c fifteenth century
Post-Medieval	Cannon battery	Castle S end	14144377	Diamond-shaped bastion at E end of parade
	Cannon battery	Brazen Ward	13904683	Bastion and gun platform at foot of sidings
	Cannon battery	N of Brazen Ward	13834694	Gun platform: at foot of sidings
	Cannon battery	N of Gannet's Rock	13584777	Gun platform: at foot of sidings
	Cannon battery	NE Point (bottom)	13514802	Gun platform: at foot of sidings
	? Guardhouse	Puffin Slope—foot of sidings	13454803	Rectangular building terraced into slope; fireplace and seat
	? Watchpoint	NE point (top)	13434793	Square foundation below plateau level at NE Point

Period	Type of site	Location	National Grid Reference	Remarks
	? Guardhouse	North End	13334789	John O'Groats. Rectangular building; fireplace and seat
	Storage chamber	S end of castle enclosure	14214374	Benson's Cave: masonry façade. Eighteenth century graffiti
Industrial	Quarry	E coast between Quarter and Halfway Walls	—	Quarries, railway, jetty and sundry buildings
Miscellaneous	Round tower	S of Threequarter Wall, east track	13584653	Either robbed burial cairn or, more probably, butt of a windmill
	Punch bowl	W side, S of Halfway Wall	13174552	? Mineral working washpan. Enclosure adjacent
	Millstones	N of Threequarter Wall, west track	13454672	Unfinished millstones and quarries on track and in west track enclosure
	Jenny's Cove IV	300 yds N of Halfway Wall, west track	13264613	Structure similar to earliest 'blackhouses' in Shetland—undated
	Standing Stones	Various	—	Of no proven significance. ? Rubbing stones. Marker stones

APPENDIX B

Owners, Administrators and Tenants of Lundy

c1140–c1150   Henry de Newmarch.

c1150–   Jordan de Marisco.

1160–1220   The Knights Templar : granted Lundy by Henry II but the de Mariscos would not yield possession.

–1194–1225   William de Marisco, son of Jordan.

1225–1234   Sir Jordan de Marisco, son of William.

1234–1242   Sir William de Marisco, son of Sir Jordan : dispossessed in 1242 when Lundy declared forfeit to the Crown due to the piracy of his father's cousin, William de Marisco (son of Geoffrey), who had installed himself on the island since 1235.

1242–1254   Lundy forfeit to the Crown (Henry III).

     1242–43   William de Rummare, Constable.

     1243   Richard de Especheleg, Constable.

     1244   William de Cantilupe, Constable.

     1245–50   Henri de Traci, Constable.

     1250–51   Robert de Walerand, Governor.

     1251–   William la Zuche, Keeper.

1254–1281   Prince Edward (eldest son of Henry III), became King 1272; William la Zuche still there October, 1254.

     –1264   Mauger de Sancto Albino, Keeper.

     1264 Sir Ralph de Wyllenton, Keeper July-September.

     1264–65   Humphrey de Bohun the Younger, Keeper.

     1265   Adam Gurdon, Keeper June-November.

     1265–66   William, Earl of Pembroke, Keeper (The King's brother).

     1266–?72   Prince Edmund, Keeper (The King's second son).

     ?1272–?74   Sir Geoffrey Dinan, Baron Dinan.

     ?1274–75   Oliver de Dinan, his son (without authority).

Page 143 : *(above)* Nesting kittiwakes; *(below)* Guillemots

Page 144 : *(above)* The resident population in 1969; Mr and Mrs F. W. Gade are seated; *(below)* Lundy ponies

	1275 Geoffrey de Shauketon, Keeper May-July.
	1275 Oliver de Dinan, lessee.
1281–1284	Sir William de Marisco restored.
1284–1289	Sir John de Marisco, his son.
1289–1290	Herbert de Marisco, his son, a minor; inheritance in the protection of the King.
	1290 Rotheric de Weylite, Custodian.
	Olivia de Marisco (widow of Sir John), claimant.
1300–1321	Olivia de Marisco.
1321–1326	Herbert de Marisco held title but not possession (died 1326).
?1321–1322	Sir John de Wyllenton, whose lands were forfeit to the Crown 1322.
1322–1326	Hugh, Lord Despencer the Younger (died 1326); grant by Edward II, deposed 1326.
1326–1327	Prince Edward, later Edward III.
	1326 William de Kerdestan, Keeper November-December.
	1326–27 Otto de Bodrigan, Keeper.
1327–	Sir John de Wyllenton, son of Sir Ralph. Estates restored.
	Stephen de Marisco, brother of Sir John de Marisco, claimant.
–1332	Sir Ralph de Wyllenton, son of Sir John de Wyllenton.
1332–1344	William de Montacute, first Earl of Salisbury. Purchased from Sir Ralph de Wyllenton, with financial settlement to all other claimants.
	John Luttrell (died 1337–8), ? lessee.
1344	William, second Earl of Salisbury, a minor. Inheritance in the protection of the King (Edward III).
	Katherine de Montacute (widow of 1st Earl), claimant to one-third of the island.
1349–?1364	William, second Earl of Salisbury. (Came of age 1349, the year his mother died).
?1364–1390	Sir Guy de Bryan, husband of Elizabeth, daughter of second Earl of Salisbury.
1390	Elizabeth de Bryan, a minor, granddaughter of Sir Guy. Inheritance in the protection of the King (Richard II).
	1391–93 John Devereux, Keeper appointed by the

	King (brother-in-law of Elizabeth de Bryan, and died 1393).
	1393–1400 John de Holand, Keeper. (Half-brother of the King).
1400–	Elizabeth Lovell (*née* Bryan) came of age 1400.
–1436	Maud Stafford (*née* Lovell), her daughter.
1436–1438	Humphrey Fitzalan, Earl of Arundel, her son, a minor (died 1438).
1438–1457	Avice Butler, Countess of Ormonde (*née* Stafford) his half-sister.
1457–1461	James Butler, 5th Earl of Ormonde, her husband. Executed 1461, lands forfeit to the Crown.
1462–1463	William Neville, Earl of Kent. By grant of his nephew, the new King, Edward IV.
1463–1478	George, Duke of Clarence, the King's brother, died 1478, estate forfeit to the King (Edward IV).
	1479–1488 John Wykes, 'Gentilman', by grant of the King.
1488–1515	Thomas Butler, 7th Earl of Ormonde, restored to his brother's estates.
1515–1532	Anne St Leger (*née* Butler), his daughter.
1532–	Sir George St Leger, her son.
–1577	Sir John St Leger, his son.
1577–1591	Mary Grenville (*née* St Leger), his daughter.
1591–	Sir Barnard Grenville, her son.
–1643	Sir Bevil Grenville, his son.
1643–1701	John Grenville, his son, later 1st Earl of Bath 1643–47 Thomas Bushell, appointed Governor by the King during the Civil War.
1647–1660	William, 1st Viscount Saye and Sele, by grant of Parliament (John Grenville, Royalist, still claimant). –1658–9– Sir John Ricketts, Commonwealth Governor.
1660	John Grenville, 1st Earl of Bath, restored (Charles II).
1701	Charles Grenville, his son.
1701–1711	William Grenville, his son, died without issue.
1711–1754	John Leveson, Lord Gower, his cousin. (Jane Grenville, daughter of the 1st Earl of Bath, married Sir William Leveson Gower). c 1720 Mr Scores, tenant farmer. 1748–1754 Thomas Benson, lessee.

1754–1775   Administered by executors of Lord Gower, died without issue.

1775–1781   Sir John Borlase Warren, by purchase.

1781–1803   John Cleveland, by purchase.
Island leased to tenants under the owner's supervision.
Two tenants were Mr Hole died 1788, and Mr Budd left in 1791.

1803–1818   Sir Vere Hunt, by purchase.

1818–1830   Sir Aubrey de Vere Hunt, his son.

1830–1834   John Matravers and W. Stiffe, his creditors.

1834–1883   William Hudson Heaven, by purchase. Resided on Lundy.
c 1850–61   Mr John Lee, tenant of the farm.
1863–1868   Lundy Granite Co, lessees of granite workings and farm.
c 1868–75   Mr Blackmore, tenant farmer.
1875–85   Mr McCarthy, tenant farmer.

1883–1916   The Rev Hudson Grosett Heaven, son of William Hudson Heaven.
1885–91   Mr Wright, tenant farmer.
1891–99   Mr Ackland, tenant farmer.
1899–1908   Mr G. T. Taylor, tenant farmer.
1908–1917   L. and W. F. Saunt, lessees of the island excepting Millcombe.

1916–1918   Walter Hudson Heaven, cousin of the Rev H. G. Heaven.
1917–1920   Mr S. T. Dennis, tenant farmer.

1918–1925   Augustus Langham Christie, by purchase.
Mr C. Herbert May, lessee.

1925–1954   Mr Martin Coles Harman, by purchase.
1940   Mr Van Os leased Lundy except for Millcombe, but remained there only a few months.

1954–1968   Albion P. Harman, Ruth Harman-Jones and Diana P. Keast son and daughters of Mr M. C. Harman, joint owners.

1968–1969   Kathleen Harman (widow of A. P. Harman) Ruth Harman-Jones and Diana P. Keast, joint owners.

1969   The National Trust : lessees, The Landmark Trust.

APPENDIX C

History of Population

1242	17	Outlaws. William de Marisco and confederates. Possibly also populated by 'civilians'.
1243	50+	The King's Constable, garrison and farm workers.
1647	21	Feb 24th. Thomas Bushell and garrison.
1655	100+	(Probably exaggerated).
1694	23	Grose. 'Housed in seven houses'.
c1795	20	Estimated. Report to Barrack Master, Barnstaple.
1813	c30	Estimated.
1851	34	(16 males and 18 females). First official census. Housed in 5 houses.
1861	48	(35 males and 13 females). In 5 houses, one new house uninhabited.
1865	240	Estimated. Opening of the quarries.
1871	144	(110 males and 34 females). In 10 houses. Also 33 uninhabited houses and 4 under construction.
1881	177	(146 males and 31 females). In 11 houses; 16 houses uninhabited and 4 under construction.
1885	61	Ward's *North Devon*.
1886	40	Approximately.
1887	43	Chanter. 'Mr Heaven, his family and establishments, farm manager and his family and servants, a few labourers, and Trinity House officials and families'.
1891	53	(26 males and 27 females). In 12 houses; 16 uninhabited houses.
1895	60	Estimated by J. L. W. Page.
1901	94	(78 males and 16 females). In 11 houses. Four houses uninhabited. This total of 15 houses compares with the total of 28 houses in 1891, showing that 13 houses at Quarter Wall were dismantled and partly used in the building of St Helena's Church.
1910	44	
1911	49	(23 males and 26 females). In 11 houses.

148

1921	48	(35 males and 13 females). In 11 houses.
1925	23	Parish Register. December 27th.
1931	21	(13 males and 8 females). In 5 houses.
1944	8	Lowest war-time figure. Agent and his wife and 6 lighthouse men.
1950	15	Resident, including lighthousemen. The maximum summer population was 75 made up of hotel guests and visitors to the Field Society.
1956	20	Including 6 lighthousemen.
1966	16	Including 6 lighthousemen.
1969	10	(5 married couples).

APPENDIX D

Two Accounts of Lundy in the Eighteenth Century

In July 1752 Thomas Benson received a party of three visitors on the island, one of whom subsequently wrote this description which was published in an issue of the *North Devon Magazine* for 1824 :

'The island at this time was in no state of improvement; the houses miserably bad; one on each side of the platform; that on the right was inhabited by Mr Benson and his friends; the other by servants. The Old Fort was occupied by the Convicts, whom he had sent there some time before, and employed in making a wall across the island; they were locked up every night when they returned from their labour. And about a week before we landed, seven or eight of them took the long-boat belonging to the island, and made their escape to Hartland, and were never heard of afterwards. Wildfowl, it being the breeding season, were exceeding plenty, and a vast number of rabbits; we employed ourselves every day in pursuit of them. The island at that time was overgrown with ferns and heath, which made it almost impassable to go over to the extreme of the island. Had it not been for the supply of rabbits and young seagulls our table would have been but poorly furnished; rats being so plenty that they destroyed every night what was left of our repast by day. Lobsters were tolerable plenty, and some other fish we caught. Mr Benson carried over some deer and goats, which increased, and were very wild and difficult to get at. The path to the house was so narrow and steep, that it was scarcely possible for a horse to ascend it. The inhabitants, by the assistance of a rope, climbed up a rock, in which were steps cut out to place their feet, up to a cave or magazine, where Mr Benson lodged his goods, and which was occasionally locked up. . . . There happened to come into the road, one evening, near twenty sail of vessels, which induced us to turn out early next morning to see them weigh their anchors, and sail. The colours were hoisted on the fort, and they all, as they passed Rat Island, returned the compliment, excepting one vessel, which provoked Mr Benson to fire at her himself, with ball, though we used every argument in our power to prevent him, urging the impropriety of it, as it might be noticed; and for our own ends, as ammunition grew scarce, for our diversion in shooting. He replied that the island was his, and every vessel that passed it and did not pay him the same compliment as was paid to the King's forts, he would fire on her. . . . He often said that the sending of the convicts to Lundy was the same as sending them to America; they were transported from England, it mattered not where it was, so as they were out of the kingdom.'

The same writer returned for a further visit in 1787 and his account of this is preceeded by an editor's note as follows:

'. . . You ascend into the island by a narrow path, just wide enough for a horse to get up, which leads you to a platform where two roads meet: one conducts you to the Castle, the other (to the house lately built by Sir John Warren) wide enough for carts, and where they land goods that are to be carried off, or brought on the island. At some small distance above the landing-place are the remains of an ancient wall, on each side of the way, supposed to be built to guard the entrance to the island, that being the only accessible point, and, it is said, that there was a chain formerly fixed there. You find on many parts of the island, where there was the least chance of landing, upwards of 40 ancient structures of stone-work, some without any cement, and others strongly united with it, on which guns were planted in Queen Anne's war with the French. . . .'

The *Journal* report itself reads:

'After dinner, we walked to view the rocks on the western part of the island, and saw vast quantities of wildfowl, (it being the breeding season) and the method of taking them in nets, which the inhabitants use, for the advantage of their feathers. The nets are made in the form of those commonly used for taking rabbits on warrens. They are fixed on the rocks, and sometimes on the ground, on stocks, in the breeding places. Every morning and evening the natives watch their nets, and take out the birds that are entangled. They catch in a good season 1,700 or 1,800, and make 1 shilling per pound of their feathers. People from the neighbouring coast are hired to pluck them, at twopence per dozen and pluck about four dozen per day.

'The birds usually taken are Muirrs, of which there are two sorts, parrots, and a small kind of gull'. The Editor adds: . . . 'The natives collect these eggs, and send to the Bristol sugar refineries. The Muirrs are the most profitable, twelve of them producing one pound of feathers. After being plucked they are skinned; these skins are

151

boiled in a furnace for the oil they yield, which is used instead of candles; and the flesh is given to the hogs, who feed on it voraciously. On returning from the rocks, our traveller observed the ruins of an old chapel, dedicated to St Helen, on the highest part of the island; some of the walls remained; the entrance, built of moorstone or spar, was from the north; its length about 25 ft, breadth 12 ft, doorway 4 ft, thickness of the walls nearly 2½ ft.'

The visitor's account continues: 'Under the west window Lord Say and Seale was supposed to be buried. Mr Hole, who had resided on the island four years, dug up the grave and deposited the bones he found in the common burial-place, which surrounds the chapel'.

The Editor comments: 'On a pleasant spot between the chapel and the house our traveller saw the ground Sir John Warren had marked out to build a handsome house on. It is supposed that he expended, in the few years he had the island, 6,000 *l*. He employed 40 labourers or menchanics yearly'. The account itself continues: '. . . We walked in the evening to the castle (or rather its site); the castle is entirely demolished. It stood on the extremity of the south part of the island, facing Hartland Point, on two acres of ground, and was surrounded by a stone wall with a ditch, excepting towards the sea, on the south, where the rock is almost perpendicular; the ditch appears very visible, and part of the walls, though most of them has been destroyed for the purpose of building offices for farming. The walls of the citadel are very perfect, of a square form; it is converted into modern dwellings. . . . In front of the house five guns are planted. The garrison was supplied with water from a spring which rises above the house built by Sir John Warren; it was conveyed from thence in earthen pipes. . . . We took a walk to the chapel, and the Beacon-hill, to determine which was the highest spot for erecting a Lighthouse, the Merchants of Bristol having offered to build one at their own expense if Mr Cleveland was agreeable . . . on examining the ground, we thought the Beacon-hill, the highest and most proper spot for the purpose. At our return, notice was sent to the castle that there would be prayers, and a sermon, next day.

'On Sunday the 8th, accordingly, prayers were read by the Rev Mr Cutcliffe, and a sermon preached by Mr Smith, to a congregation of 22 persons. . . . The northern part is very barren and rocky; . . . on our return (from the north end) I saw the remains of a windmill. The north part is now incapable of being improved, from Mr Benson's setting the heath and ferns on fire, while he was in possession, so that the earth continued burning for some days, till it came to the bare rock, and now nothing vegetable grows on it. . . . Springs abound in many parts of the island, the water in general very soft, clear, and pleasant to the taste, and no way brackish. There was another pond between the beacon and the chapel.'

APPENDIX E

The Stamps of Lundy

Lundy stamps are issued in Puffin values, a Puffin equalling 1d. The initial rates for 'puffinage' were : first 2 oz, ½ puffin; subsequent 2 oz, 1 puffin.

There have been several issues of Lundy stamps, and some overprints of existing stamps. Numerous printer's proofs, colour experiments and imperforate trials exist but the stamps detailed below are the only ones which have been officially issued. (All those issues of which such trials exist are mentioned below).

1929 Issue

First delivery	10.3.29
First Issue	1.11.29

Printed by Bradbury Wilkinson & Co Ltd in sheets of 120 stamps, each sheet having four panels of 30 stamps.

½ puffin red	500,000
1 puffin blue	500,000

The need for stamps of higher-values led to the

1930 Issue

First issue due 1.6.30 but not delivered until 11.7.30. Printed by Bradbury Wilkinson & Co, Ltd in sheets of 120 stamps, each sheet having four panels of 30 stamps.

6 puffin mauve	250,000
9 puffin brown	250,000
12 puffin green	250,000

John D. Stanard, writing in *Lundy Island—A Philatelic Handbook* in 1938, said that the initial printing of 12,000 6 p stamps was in blue and the subsequent printing in mauve. This is not confirmed and it seems likely that any blue 6 p stamps have been overexposed to sunlight and have faded. All the above stamps are without watermark and the perforation is twelve, all round.

On 1 June 1934 Mr R. T. Boyd started an experimental air mail service which became a regular service on 1.4.35 with the name

154

of Atlantic Coast Air Services. This service was a private one and the stamps issued for it do not have puffin values. The first printing of stamps for the air service was in the form of a small label, and these are often referred to as 'Tramticket varieties' :

1935 Atlantic Coast Air Services Issue
All printed in rolls of 500 by Willsons Ltd of Leicester.

$\frac{1}{2}$d black on red. Nos 00001 to 04000. First printing 1.4.35, withdrawn 20.12.35. Also inverted 'T' for 1 and fraction bar.

$\frac{1}{2}$d black on red. Nos 04001 to 06000. 6,000 printed, 12 rolls in all. Second printing 3.5.35, withdrawn 1.4.36. Also inverted 'T' for 1 and fraction bar.

1d black on yellow. Nos 00001 to 02000. 2,000 printed, 4 rolls in all. Printed 3.12.35, withdrawn 1.4.36.

3d black on blue. Nos 00001 to 02000. First printing 1.4.35, withdrawn 20.12.35. Nos 02001 to 04000. Second printing 3.12.35, withdrawn 1.4.36. 4,000 printed, 8 rolls in all.

The second series of Atlantic Coast Air Services stamps followed the withdrawal of the tramticket series :

1936 Atlantic Coast Air Services Issue
Printed by H. Pincombe & Son of Ilfracombe, 28.3.36, in sheets of twelve and bound in books of 100 sheets. 12,000 of each value (10 books) issued 1.4.36.
Rouletted.

| $\frac{1}{2}$d black | 1d red | 6d orange |
| 1d red | 3d blue | 1s lavender |

On 26.4.37 the Lundy & Atlantic Coast Air Lines Ltd was registered as a public company with Mr Boyd, the pilot, and Mr Gade, the agent, as directors and Mr W. J. Boyd as secretary. For this undertaking a smaller stamp was printed showing an aerial view of the island with an aeroplane and the word 'Lundy' just above the aeroplane. Of these stamps 24,000 were printed on 11.6.37 but were not issued for sale as Mr Harman did not want it to be thought or suggested that the air service conducted by Mr Boyd was owned by the Lundy Island authority. Accordingly, a second printing of 24,000 was made by Willsons of the same design but with the words Lundy & Atlantic Coast Airlines Ltd around the design. These stamps appeared on 22 July 1937. The original borderless variety were used on Lundy for incoming mail only.

Also stamps with printing irregularities.

LUNDY

1937 Lundy & Atlantic Coasts Airlines Issue

½d violet 24,000 issued in sheets of 48. Also with printing irregularities .

The ½d and 1d of the 1936 issue were withdrawn on the introduction of the 1937 issue.

1938 Lundy & Atlantic Coasts Air Lines Ltd Issue

Owing to a shortage of the 1937 issue, some of the borderless variety mentioned above were overprinted Lundy and Atlantic Coasts Air Lines Ltd in four lines in black, and issued on 1.11.38.

½d violet borderless overprint 5,328 issued. Also variation Atlantic mis-spelt.

1939 Lundy and Atlantic Coasts Air Lines Ltd Issue

The previous design was used for the ½d value and a new design of an aeroplane circling the Old Light used for the 1d value. Issued 31.3.39.

½d bright red   96,000 printed
1d black   48,000 printed
Also printing irregularities.

1939 Additional Issue

Printed by Bradbury Wilkinson Ltd, all of the same design, in sheets of 60 stamps, each having two panels of 30.

2p grey-blue   100,000 printed   Issued 1.11.39
3p black   100,000 printed   Issued 1.11.39
4p pink   100,000 printed   Issued 1.11.39
This was the first issue of Lundy stamps since 1930.

1939 Anniversary Overprint

To commemorate the 10th anniversary of the issue of Lundy stamps, the five original values were overprinted by Bradbury Wilkinson Ltd.

Overprint '1929–1939'. Issued 1.11.39, 5,400 issued of each.

½p red over red   9p red over brown
1p red over blue   12p red over green
6p red over mauve

1940 Red Cross Overprint

Mr T. Rigby Hall suggested that Lundy stamps could be used to raise funds for the Red Cross by surcharging them and selling

156

them at double their face value. Mr Harman agreed but stipulated a date after which all unsold stamps so treated were to be destroyed.

Overprinted by Dalkeith Press Ltd.
Overprint 'Red Cross Surtax –p.' with a cross.
Values ½p, 1p, 2p, 10,000 each issued.
Values remaining 5,000 each issued.

½p red over red	4p red over pink
1p red over blue	6p red over mauve
2p red over grey-blue	9p red over brown
3p red over black	12p red over green

Also printing irregularity, inverted 'U' in puffin on overprint.

By this time the demand for Lundy stamps was increasing and, late in 1941, Mr Harman instituted the Lundy Philatelic Bureau, the purpose of which was to provide collectors with details and specimens of the Lundy issues. Mr T. Rigby Hall was in charge of the bureau and in the subsequent years a number of overprintings were made.

1942 Victory Overprint

All eight values were overprinted with a fighter aeroplane and a V for Victory sign. Issued 1.1.42. Overprinted by Dalkeith Press Ltd.

½p	30,000	overprinted	ultramarine
			green
			blue
			deep ultramarine
1p	13,200	overprinted	magenta
			violet
			carmine
2p	27,900	overprinted	**red**
			scarlet
3p	13,200	overprinted	green
			carmine
			emerald
4p	6,000	overprinted	black
6p	6,000	overprinted	green
			emerald
			carmine
9p	6,000	overprinted	green
			emerald

157

12p   6,000 overprinted   claret
red
scarlet
chocolate

Also many colour variations and imperforates exist other than the official colours above.

1943 Tighearna Sheet Issue

Issued 1.2.43. Printed by Dalkeith Press Ltd. Miniature sheet of four stamps (two ½p, one 2p, one 9p,) retailing at 1s with the title 'Tighearna'. Issued to commemorate the Stone of Tigernus in the cemetery. The 2p value is blue compared with the grey-blue of the perforate issue. Many of the sheets were unsold and so the following stamps appeared, cut from the original sheets :

Imperforate : ½p red
2p blue
9p brown
Also various printing irregularities.

1943 Ninth Anniversary Overprint

Issued February 1943 to commemorate the 9th anniversary of the air mail service to Lundy. Overprinted by Dalkieth Press Ltd.

Overprint in gold shows a civil aeroplane and 'IX Anniversary', with a gold border around the stamp. Many unused Tighearna blocks were overprinted in this way and perforated, though not all had the gold border.
½p overprinted in gold, with border
½p overprinted in gold, without border
1p overprinted in gold, with border
2p grey-blue overprinted in gold with border
2p blue overprinted in gold without border
3p black overprinted in gold with border
4p pink overprinted in gold with border
6p mauve overprinted in gold with border
9p brown overprinted in gold without border
9p brown overprinted in gold with border
12p green overprinted in gold with border

1943 Additional Values Issue

Issued April 1943.

1½p in red over 12p green
2½p in red over 6p mauve

158

1943 Wright Brothers Overprint

Issued September 1943. The original five values ($\frac{1}{2}$p, 1p, 6p, 9p, 12p,) were overprinted with a replica of the Wright Brothers aeroplane and the figures '1903–1943'. The five values were surcharged with twelve different values.

$\frac{1}{2}$p and figures black, plane red, over 12p green
1p and figures black, plane red, over 6p mauve
1$\frac{1}{2}$p and figures green, plane black, over 9p brown
2p and figures green, plane black over 6p mauve
3p and figures orange, plane black, over 9p brown
4p and figures green, plane black, over $\frac{1}{2}$p red
5p and figures blue, plane black, over 12p green
6p figures and plane black, over 1p blue
7p and figures orange, plane black, over 6p mauve
8p and figures red, plane black, over 12p green
9p and figures red, plane black, over 1p blue
12p figures and plane black, over $\frac{1}{2}$p red

This was the last issue made by the Lundy Philatelic Bureau which closed at the end of the war in 1945. Some essays had been prepared during 1942 and 1943 but were not used :

10p : larger than the 9p but similar in design.
30p : a large stamp with outer design taken from 9p, with a puffin head design taken from the $\frac{1}{2}$p value and inset at the upper left of the design.
3p : Wright Brothers. Large stamp showing modern four-engined plane with the Wright Brothers' biplane inset at the centre.

1950 'By Air' Overprint

The air mail service to Lundy was resumed on 8.11.50 and was run by the Island authority. The original eight values were overprinted 'By Air' in black by the Gazette Printing Service of Bideford.

$\frac{1}{2}$p	12,000	4p	6,000
1p	12,000	6p	4,000
2p	6,000	9p	2,200
3p	6,000	12p	1,000

1951 Issue

With the withdrawal of sea transport in this year, a new series of charges was made for postage. Six new values were issued and also the original ½p value was replaced, making seven new designs in all. Designed by John Dyke. Printed by Harrison & Sons Ltd. Sheets of 48 in two panels of 24. 100,000 printed in each value.

½p pink, Puffin	5p orange, Fulmer Petrel
1½p green, Guillemot	7p black, Oyster Catcher
2½p blue, Kittiwake	7½p brown, Gt. Black-backed Gull
3½p red, Razorbill	

An eight-Puffin value was needed and the large stock of 12p stamps was used for overprinting.

8p overprinted on 12p green. 38,250 issued.

8p and 'By Air' overprinted on 12p green. 1951 3-bar deletion of 12p. 2,000 issued. 1953 2-bar deletion of 12p. 3,000 issued.

Also colour trials of overprintings.

1953 Coronation Overprint

Five original values overprinted 'Coronation 2.6.1953'; 240,000 of each value issued.

½p overprinted in black 'Coronation 2.6.1953'
1p overprinted in red 'Coronation 2.6.1953'
2p overprinted in red 'Coronation 2.6.1953 By Air'
4p overprinted in black 'Coronation 2.6.1953 By Air'
6p overprinted in black 'Coronation 2.6.1953'
9p overprinted in black 'Coronation 2.6.1953'
12p overprinted in black 'Coronation 2.6.1953'

1954 Jubilee Issue

On 1.1.54 a new series of regular and air mail stamps were issued to commemorate the 25th anniversary of the first issue of Lundy stamps. These were the first multicoloured pictorials issued. Designed by John Dyke. Printed by Harrison & Sons Ltd, in sheets of 20. Withdrawn 31.12.54.

Regular :		
	½p black and magenta	500,000
	1p black and blue	500,000
	2p black and vermilion	500,000
	4p black and green	500,000
	6p black and yellow	200,000
	9p black and red	
	head and value blue	200,000
	12p blue-green and sepia	
	head and value red	200,000

Airmail :	½p blue-grey and carmine	500,000
	1p brown and blue	500,000
	2p brown and green	500,000
	3p purple and blue	200,000
	6p blue-grey and red	200,000
	12p maroon and grey	200,000

1954 Air Mail Pictorials Issue

These stamps were issued on 1.1.54 and were intended to replace all previous issues. They are similar in appearance and values to the 1954 Jubilee airmail series, except that the colours have been reversed; 200,000 of each value printed.

1955 Millenary Issues

Originally intended for issue in 1954 but delayed owing to the sudden death of Mr M. C. Harman. They commemorate the death of Eric Bloodaxe in 954, a Norseman but not connected with Lundy.

Regular :	½p mauve and green	Triangular
	1p brown and ochre	Triangular
	2p brown and blue-green	Triangular
	3p black and blue	Rhomboid
	4p blue and scarlet	Triangular
	6p black and violet	Triangular
	9p black and vermilion	Triangular
Airmail :	½p mauve and black	Triangular
	1p light and dark brown	Triangular
	2p dark green and brown	Triangular
	3p black and red	Rhomboid
	4p red and dark blue	Triangular
	6p violet and black	Triangular
	9p orange and black	Triangular

1957 Issue

Definitive issue of ordinary mail stamps. Issued 11.2.57. There is no longer an airmail service and mails are carried by the island boat, the *Lundy Gannet*, to and from Bideford.

Designed and printed by Bradbury Wilkinson & Co Ltd.

1p pink	150,000
2p green	100,000
3p blue	100,000
4p black	80,000
6p red	35,000
9p violet	35,000

LUNDY

1961 Europa Overprint

Issued 8.12.61. All nine regular issues of the 1955 Millenary values were overprinted in black with 'Europa 1961'; 500,000 sets overprinted.

Also 25,000 1p overprints were made for ordinary Lundy postal purposes.

First Day Cover dated 28.12.61 utilised one printed sheet of all the values, imperforate; 80,000 issued.

1962 Anti-Malaria Campaign Issue

Issued 25.4.62 to commemorate the world-wide campaign to which Lundy contributed. Large diamond shape; 200,000 sets printed plus 20,000 1p values for Lundy postage purposes.

    ½p dark green on stone. Knight Templar rock
    1p black on blue. Head of southern puffin
    2p brown on green. Peregrine falcon
    3p brown on grey. Head of Lundy pony
    6p mauve on pink. Old Light
    12p black on terracotta. Mosquito at rest
This issue withdrawn mid-August 1962.

1962 Europa Issue

Issued end September 1962. Four values perforate :

    1p blue on pink
    2p brown on blue
    6p brown on yellow
    9p black on green
    2,000 imperforate sets were also issued.

From 1 April 1964 the rates for 'puffinage' were changed. Postcards remained at one puffin, but letters up to eight ounces in weight were charged at two puffins.

1964 Shakespeare Quarter Centenary Issue

Issued 27.7.64. Three values of similar appearance showing a bust of the poet, with a falcon in flight over Lundy.

2p green	40,000
10p pink	30,000
18p blue	30,000

1965 'One Puffin' Overprint

By 1965 the 1p value of the 1957 definitive issue was exhausted and so 18,000 of the 3p blue of 1957 were overprinted for use as

162

1p. Issued 3.4.65, no first-day covers. Overprinted by Gazette Printing Service.

1965 Churchill Commemorative Issue

Issued 29.6.65. Three values of similar appearance showing portrait of Sir Winston Churchill with a view of Lundy in the background.

    2p purple and orange
    10p deep blue and magenta
    18p black and violet

1967 'Help Save Seabirds from Oil' Issue

Issued 29.5.67. A block of four stamps, each of 6-puffin denomination, the text of each printed in a different language—English, French, German and Dutch. Printed by Thos. de la Rue in four colours showing nesting puffins overlooking sea being polluted by a tanker. The proceeds of sale of these stamps during 1967 was handed jointly to the British RSPCA and the International ISPA to assist their work in saving seabirds from the effects of oil pollution.

1969 One Puffin Overprint

By the summer of 1969 the 1-puffin value of the 1929 definitive issue was exhausted and so 11,760 of the 9p brown of 1930 were overprinted for use as 1p. Issued 11.8.69. No first-day covers. Overprinting undertaken by John Dyke, using silkscreen process.

1969 Postal Anniversary Issue

Issued 1.11.69 to commemorate the 40th anniversary of Lundy's first stamp issue. Designed by John Dyke and printed in sheets of 30 stamps by Bradbury, Wilkinson & Co Ltd.

    1p grey showing 'Postmaster Allday and Lundy Mails 1912'
    2p orange-brown showing *Lundy Gannet*
    6p light blue showing the skiff *Gannet*
    9p turquoise-green showing the *Lerina*
    12p pale violet showing the 'Rapide' aeroplane

20,000 of each value were printed, plus an additional 20,000 of the 1p and 2p varieties. 2,500 first-day covers were prepared.

Lundy Franking Stamps

A variety of franking stamps have been used on Lundy. These are itemised below in chronological order :

7.12.1886	GPO issued a single line circle metal stamp to Cardiff Post Office. This had 'Lundy Island' at the top with initial C below, month and day, and year at the bottom. (Examples of this exist before the service opened on 4.3.1887).
4.8.1893	Barnstaple was assigned the same type as above but with A instead of C below Lundy Island.
31.7.1909	An oval-shaped single line postmark was issued to the Coast Guard with 'Lundy Island' at the top and an asterisk on either side and 'Coast Guard' at the bottom.
1927–1929	Unstamped, unfranked mail.
March 1929	The first private cancellation used was a small rectangular single line postmark with a line near the centre from top to bottom. The left half showed a standing puffin and the right half had 'Lundy' at top and bottom with date in the centre. Usually black ink, but red and green were also used sometimes.
1929–1938	Rubber franking stamp inscribed 'Lundy' with the date within a circle. Green ink used.
1939–1943	Rectangular stamp inscribed 'Lundy Lights and Leads' with the figure of a puffin but no date. Green or black ink.
1937	Used by the Atlantic Coast Air Services, oblong with a symbolic drawing of a wing, together with the date and 'Barnstaple' and 'Lundy Island'. Blue ink.
1937	Lundy and Atlantic Coast Airlines used a single circle cancellation with 'Air' at the top, 'L.A.C.A.L.' in the centre and 'Post' at the bottom. Blue or black ink.
1938–1939	On 1.11.1938 the 'Air' and 'Post' were cut out of the stamp used by the Lundy and Atlantic Coast Airlines. Purple, blue or black ink cancellations.
1942	'Bureau Mail' franking stamp. Used by the Lundy Philatelic Bureau on its correspondence. 'Bureau Mail' flanked by a series of horizontal lines. Black ink.
1943	On 1.9.43 a special round single line circle postmark was used with 'Lundy' around the top, the Wright Brothers' biplane next and '1.9.43 First Day of Issue' at bottom.
1943–1950	Circular metal franking stamp inscribed 'Lundy' both above and below the date. Blue or black ink. This

stamp has been used since 1943 with the exception of the franking stamps mentioned below.

1950–1952 A rubber stamp of large rectangular design was used for cancellation of the airmail stamps during the period when both sea and air services ran concurcurrently. This was inscribed 'Lundy Air Post Lundy Air Post' with the date and a puffin in flight. Black, or more rarely blue, ink.

On cessation of seaborne mail, the metal stamp mentioned above was used on all mail.

1953 One-day Coronation franking stamp. Circular metal stamp inscribed 'Lundy Coronation 2 June 1953 God Save The Queen'. Black ink.

1954 Circular metal stamp inscribed 'Lundy Jubilee Year' with the date. Black or green ink.

1955–1957 Circular metal stamp inscribed 'Lundy Millenary' with the date. Black ink.

1961–1962 Circular single line mark inscribed 'Lundy' at top, date in the middle, and 'Europa' at the bottom. This was used for the 1961 and 1962 issues. Black ink.

Delayed By Storm. During the winter of 1961–62 an oval mark was introduced and stamped on mail from Lundy which had been delayed by adverse weather. Single line oval metal stamp inscribed 'Delayed by Storm' around the edge and 'Lundy' in the middle.

No date. Black ink.

1962 April-August. Circular single line mark inscribed 'Lundy' at top, date in the middle and 'Anti-Malaria' at the bottom. This stamp was not ready in time for the first-day covers, which were cancelled with a rubber stamp which tended to give smudged details. Black ink.

1964 Circular single line mark inscribed 'Lundy' at top, the date in the middle, and with a blank space at the bottom.

APPENDIX F

The Lundy Golf Course

The fascinating story of the Lundy golf course was fully told by Mr F. W. Gade in the third issue of the *Lundy Review* (1958). In 1960, thirty-two years after the course had been abandoned, Mr Gade was still able to trace the following details of it, shown on the accompanying map. The nine-hole course was laid out on the site known as Ackland's Moor, immediately north of the Old Light and on the western side of the plateau.

Hole 1. Tee near Old Light. Ladies' tee about 50 ft due north.

Green : the 'arrow banks' of the green are curved westerly and are obvious, with stones on top. They are a little east of a stream.

Hole 2. Tee 75 ft south-west of 'arrow banks'; 10 ft west of a path.

Green : about 40 yd east-south-east of telegraph pole 30.

Hole 3. Tee about 40 yd almost due east of telegraph pole 30.

Green : about 75 yd south of high pond, on edge of bracken.

Hole 4. Tee 25 yd south-east of third green.

Green : slightly raised, circular, 20 yd to south-east.

Hole 5. Tee about 20 yd due north of fourth green, by Quarter Wall and very clearly marked.

Green : 90 yd due east in angle of wall.

Hole 6. Tee in line between fifth green and Old Light, about 40–50 yd from fifth green.

Green : 15 yd due west of broken wall—overgrown by bracken.

Hole 7. Tee approximately 50 yd due north of rubble, near a wall which runs north.

Green : near aircraft ditch and hump.

Hole 8. Tee 75 yd north-east of 'arrow banks'.

Green : unmarked but, by character of land probably 75 yd due north of ninth tee.

Hole 9. Tee also unmarked but probably 75 yd north of Lighthouse Field Wall, 10 yd west of north-running wall. Ground very flat.

Green : raised, obvious, near old hut at Old Light.

'Bogey' for the course was 36. Bunkers were to have been created later but never materialised. The course was officially opened on 29 July 1920 but abandoned at the end of the 1928 season. The first and only greenkeeper-professional was Mr Ivor Llewellyn.

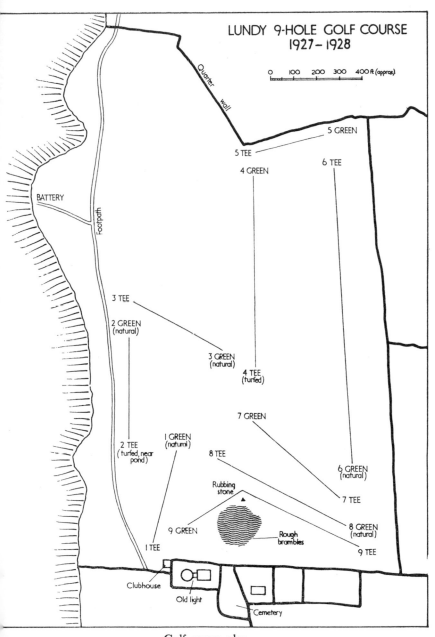

Golf course plan

APPENDIX G

Minerals recorded on Lundy

Beryl	In small white-yellow columnar crystals.
Felspar	In white tubular crystals.
Fluor	Crystallised and massive.
Garnet	
Mica	In plates, and hexagonal crystals.
Rock Crystal	Transparent, frequently dark brown or black.
Schorl	
China Clay	Formed from disintegrating felspar, is present in small quantities but is too impregnated with iron to be useful.

In the slate are veins and strings of *Gossan* containing :

Blende	Sulphuret of zinc, traces.
Towanite	Copper pyrities.
Magnetite	Magnetic iron ore, found in a vein below Benjamin's Chair.
Quartz	Amorphous and crystalline, is found in veins crossing the slate in every direction and seems to be the most abundant non-metallic mineral.
Limestone	A seam appears on the beach and passes south-eastwards through Hell's Gates. This fault of a soluble mineral may well account for the separation of Rat Island from the main island.

The Flora of Lundy

Flowering Plants and Deciduous Trees

Water crowfoot	*Ranunculus lenormandi*
Ivy-leaved crowfoot	*R. hederaceus*
Great spearwort	*R. lingua*
Lesser spearwort	*R. flammula*
Meadow crowfoot	*R. acris*
Creeping buttercup	*R. repens*
Bulbous buttercup	*R. bulbosus*
Lesser celandine	*R. ficaria*
Marsh marigold	*Caltha palustris*
Common columbine	*Aquilegia vulgaris*
Opium poppy	*Papaver somniferum*
Ramping fumitory	*Fumaria bastardii*
Wallflower	*Cheiranthus cheiri*
Common watercress	*Nasturtium officinale*
Hairy bitter cress	*Cardamine hirsuta*
Sweet alyssum	*Lobularia maritima*
Common scurvy grass	*Cochlearia officinalis*
Danish scurvy grass	*C. danica*
English scurvy grass	*C. anglica*
Thale rock cress	*Arabidopsis thaliana*
Common hedge mustard	*Sisymbrium officinale*
Flixweed	*S. orientale*
Common wild navew	*Brassica napus*
Lundy cabbage	*Rhyncosinapis wrightii*
Charlock	*Sinapis arvensis*
Sand rocket	*Diplotaxis muralis*
Shepherd's purse	*Capsella bursa-pastoris*
Lesser wart cress	*Coronopus didymus*
Swine cress	*C. squamatus*
Broad-leaved pepper-wort	*Cardaria draba*
Hairy pepper-wort	*Lepidium smithii*
Narrow-stalked teesdalia	*Teesdalia nudicaulis*
Wild mignonette	*Reseda lutea*

Dyer's rocket	*R. luteola*
Common rock-rose	*Helianthemum chamaecistus*
Dog violet I	*Viola riviniana*
Dog violet II	*V. canina*
Marsh violet	*V. palustris*
Heartsease	*V. tricolor*
Common milkwort	*Polygala vulgaris*
Heath milkwort	*P. serpyllifolia*
Milkwort	*P. oxyptera*
Deptford pink	*Dianthus armeria*
Bladder campion	*Silene cucubalus*
Sea campion	*S. maritima*
English catchfly	*S. anglica*
Evening campion, or White campion	*Melandrium alba*
Red campion	*M. rubrum*
Ragged robin	*Lychnis flos-cuculi*
Corn cockle	*Agrostemina githago*
Sea mouse-ear chickweed	*Cerastium tetrandum*
Mouse-ear chickweed	*C. vulgatum*
Mouse-ear chickweed, var.	*C. tomentosum*
Chickweed	*Stellaria media*
Greater stitchwort	*S. holostea*
Lesser stitchwort	*S. graminea*
Bog stitchwort	*S. alsine*
Sea purslane	*Honkenya peploides*
Sea pearl-wort	*Sagina maritima*
Annual pearl-wort	*S. apetala*
Sciliated pearl-wort	*S. ciliata*
Reuter's pearl-wort	*S. c. reuteri*
Procumbent pearl-wort	*S. procumbens*
Corn spurrey	*Spergula arvensis*
Sea spurrey	*Spergularia salina*
Rock spurrey	*S. rupicola*
Rock spurrey, var.	*S. marginata*
Sand spurrey	*S. rubra*
Water blinks	*Montia verna*
Tamarisk	*Tamarix gallica*
Common tutsan	*Hypericum androsaemum*
Perforate St. John's wort	*H. perforatum*
Trailing St. John's wort	*H. humifusum*
Slender St. John's wort	*H. pulchrum*

Marsh St. John's wort	*H. elodes*
Musk mallow	*Malva moschata*
Common mallow	*M. sylvestris*
Common lime	*Tilia platyphylla*
All seed	*Radiola linoides*
Common flax	*Linum usitatissimum*
Dove's-foot crane's-bill	*Geranium molle*
Small-flowered crane's-bill	*G. pusillum*
Herb robert	*G. robertianum*
Sea stork's bill	*Erodium maritimum*
Holly	*Ilex aquifolium*
Sycamore	*Acer pseudo-platanus*
Dyer's green-weed	*Genista tinctoria*
Common furze	*Ulex europaeus*
Western furze	*U. gallii*
Common broom	*Sarothamnus scoparius*
Common broom, var.	*S. sp. prostatus*
Common rest-harrow	*Ononis repens*
Bird's-foot fenugreek	*Trigonella ornithopodoides*
Black medick, or Nonsuch	*Medicago lupulina*
Lesser yellow melilot	*Melilotus altissima*
Purple clover	*Trifolium pratense*
Hare's-foot clover	*T. arvense*
Soft knotted trefoil	*T. striatum*
White or Dutch clover	*T. repens*
Hop clover	*T. campestre*
Lesser clover	*T. dubium*
Slender clover	*T. micranthum*
Common lady's fingers	*Anthyllis vulneraria*
Bird's-foot trefoil	*Lotus corniculatus*
Greater bird's-foot trefoil	*L. uliginosus*
Hispid bird's-foot trefoil	*L. hispidus*
Common bird's-foot	*Ornithopus perpusillus*
Tufted vetch	*Vicia cracca*
Common vetch	*V. sativa*
Narrow-leaved vetch	*V. angustifolia*
Spring vetch	*V. lathyroides*
Meadow pea	*Lathyrus pratensis*
Sloe, or Blackthorn	*Prunus spinosa*
Dropwort	*Filipendula vulgaris*
Blackberry	*Rubus fruticosus agg.*
Dewberry	*R. caesius*

Tormentil	*Potentilla erecta*
Creeping tormentil	*P. procumbens*
Spring cinquefoil	*P. tabernaemontani*
Creeping cinquefoil	*P. reptans*
Silver-weed	*P. anserina*
Strawberry-leaved cinquefoil	*P. sterilis*
Burnet rose	*Rosa spinosissima*
Sweet brier	*R. rubiginosa*
Mountain ash	*Sorbus aucuparia*
Crab apple	*Malus sylvestris*
Hawthorn	*Crataegus monogyna*
London pride	*Saxifraga spathularis umbrosa*
Wall pennywort	*Umbilicus rupestris*
English stonecrop	*Sedum anglicum*
Round-leaved sundew	*Drosera rotundifolia*
Water star-wort	*Callitriche stagnalis*
Water purslane	*Peplis portula*
Purple loosestrife	*Lythrum salicaria*
Broad smooth-leaved willow herb	*Epilobium montanum*
Short-podded square-stalked willow herb	*E. obscurum*
Common evening primrose	*Oenothera biennis*
Marsh pennywort	*Hydrocotyle vulgaris*
Common hemlock	*Conium maculatum*
Common marsh-wort	*Apium nodiflorum*
Corn parsley	*Petroselinum segetum*
Pig-nut	*Conopodium majus*
Sea samphire	*Crithmum maritimum*
Fool's parsley	*Aethusa cynapium*
Garden angelica	*Angelica archangelica*
Cow parsnip	*Heracleum spondylium*
Wild carrot	*Daucus carota*
Common ivy	*Hedera helix*
Common elder	*Sambucus nigra*
Wayfaring tree	*Viburnum lantana*
Snow berry	*Symphoricarpos rivularis*
Honeysuckle	*Lonicera periclymenum*
Wild madder	*Rubia peregrina*
Lady's bedstraw	*Galium verum*
Heath bedstraw	*G. hercynicum*
Water bedstraw	*G. palustre*

Rough marsh bedstraw	*G. uliginosum*
Goose grass	*G. aparine*
Red spur valerian	*Kentranthus ruber*
Devil's-bit scabious	*Succisa pratensis*
Field scabious	*Knautia arvensis*
Common hemp agrimony	*Eupatorium cannabinum*
Golden rod	*Solidago virgaurea*
Common daisy	*Bellis perennis*
Canadian flea-bane	*Erigeron candensis*
Blue flea-bane	*E. acris*
Common filago	*Filago germanica*
Marsh cudweed	*Gnaphalium uliginosum*
Common flea-bane	*Pulicaria dysenterica*
Common yarrow	*Achillea millefolium*
Sneeze-wort	*A. ptarmica*
Stinking chamomile	*Anthemis cotula*
White ox-eye	*Chrysanthemum leucanthemum*
Common feverfew or Bachelor's buttons	*C. parthenium*
Corn feverfew or Scentless mayweed	*Matricaria maritima*
Sea feverfew	*M. maritima Ssp. inodora*
Wild chamomile	*M. chamomilla*
Colt's-foot	*Tussilago farfara*
Cherry-pie	*Petasites fragrans*
Common groundsel	*Senecio vulgaris*
Mountain groundsel	*S. sylvaticus*
Hoary rag-wort	*S. erucifolius*
Common rag-wort	*S. jacobaea*
Slender-flowered thistle	*Carduus tenuiflorus*
Spear plume-thistle	*Cirsium vulgare*
Marsh plume-thistle	*C. palustre*
Meadow plume-thistle	*C. dissectum*
Creeping plume-thistle	*C. arvense*
Scotch thistle	*Onopordon acanthium*
Black knap-weed (agg.)	*Centaurea nigra*
Corn blue-bottle	*C. cyanus*
Wild chicory	*Cichorium intybus*
Common nipple-wort	*Lapsana communis*
Hawk-weed picris	*Picris hieracioides*
Bristly ox-tongue	*P. echioides*
Smooth hawk's-beard	*Crepis capillaris*

173

Narrow-leaved hawk's beard	*Hieracium umbellatum*
Mouse-ear hawk-weed	*H. pilosella*
Long-rooted cat's-ear	*Hypochaeris radicata*
Hairy hawk-bit	*Leontodon leysseri*
Rough hawk-bit	*L. hispidus*
Autumnal hawk-bit	*L. autumnalis*
Common dandelion	*Taraxacum officinale agg.*
Common sow-thistle	*Sonchus oleraceus*
Rough sow-thistle	*S. asper*
Corn sow-thistle	*S. arvensis*
Sheep's scabious	*Jasione montana*
Ivy-leaved bell-flower	*Wahlenbergia hederacea*
Ling, or Heather	*Calluna vulgaris*
Cross-leaved heath	*Erica tetralix*
Fine-leaved heath, or Bell Heather	*E. cinerea*
Sea lavender	*Limonium binervosum*
Thrift	*Armeria maritima*
Primrose	*Primula vulgaris*
Yellow pimpernel	*Lysimachia nemorum*
Sea-milkwort	*Glaux maritima*
Scarlet pimpernel	*Anagallis arvensis*
Scarlet pimpernel (white)	*A. a. var. carnea*
Scarlet pimpernel (blue)	*A. a. var. coerulea*
Bog pimpernel	*A. tenella*
Chaffweed	*Centunculus minimus*
Brookweed	*Samolus valerandi*
Ash	*Fraxinus excelsior*
Privet	*Ligustrum vulgare*
Common centaury	*Cantaurium umbellatum*
Dwarf centuary	*C. pulchellum*
Tufted centuary	*C. latifolium*
Common hound's-tongue	*Cynoglossum officinale*
Common borage	*Borago officinalis*
Tufted water scorpion-grass	*Myosotis caespitosa*
Creeping water scorpion-grass	*Myosotis secunda*
Field scorpion-grass	*M. arvensis*
Early field scorpion-grass	*M. hispida*
Parti-coloured scorpion-grass	*M. discolor*
Great bindweed	*Calystegia sepium*
Field bindweed	*Convolvulus arvensis*
Lesser dodder	*Cuscuta epithymum*

Woody nightshade	*Solanum dulcamara*
Black nightshade	*S. nigrum*
Thorn-apple	*Datura stramonium*
Common henbane	*Hyoscyamus niger*
Moth mullein	*Verbascum blattaria*
Ivy-leaved toad-flax	*Cymbalaria muralis*
Great snapdragon	*Antirrhinum majus*
Water fig-wort	*Scrophularia aquatica*
Knotted fig-wort	*S. nodosa*
Balm-leaved fig-wort	*S. scorodonia*
Purple foxglove	*Digitalis purpurea*
Field speedwell	*Veronica agrestis*
Buxbaum's speedwell	*V. persica*
Wall speedwell	*V. arvensis*
Thyme-leaved speedwell	*V. serpyllifolia*
Common speedwell	*V. officinalis*
Germander speedwell	*V. chamaedrys*
Brooklime	*V. beccabunga*
Eye-bright	*Euphrasia occidentalis*
Dwarf red-rattle	*Pedicularis sylvatica*
Yellow rattle	*Rhinanthus minor*
Great broom-rape	*Orobanche rapum-genistae*
Common vervain	*Verbena officinalis*
Marsh whorled mint	*Mentha verticillata*
Wild thyme	*Thymus serpyllum*
Ground ivy	*Glechoma hederacea*
Greater skull-cap	*Scutellaria galericulata*
Lesser skull-cap	*S. minor*
Self-heal	*Prunella vulgaris*
White horehound	*Marrubium vulgare*
Wood betony	*Stachys officinalis*
Red dead-nettle	*Lamium purpureum*
White dead-nettle	*L. album*
Wood germander	*Teucrium scorodonia*
Buck's-horn plantain	*Plantago coronopus*
Sea plantain	*P. maritima*
Ribwort plantain	*P. lanceolata*
Hoary plantain	*P. media*
Greater plantain	*P. major*
White goose-foot	*Chenopodium album*
White goose-foot, var.	*C. a. viride*

175

Good King Henry, or Sea spinach	*C. bonus-henricus*
Sea-beet	*Beta vulgaris Ssp. maritima*
Common orache	*Atriplex patula*
Common orache, var.	*A. hastata*
Common orache, var.	*A. glabriuscula*
Climbing persicaria	*Polygonum convolvulus*
Climbing persicaria, var.	*P. c. subalatum*
Common knot-grass	*P. aviculare*
Common knot-grass	*P. aequale*
Water-pepper	*P. hydropiper*
Spotted persicaria	*P. persicaria*
Pale persicaria, var.	*P. lapathifolium x persicaria*
Common buckwheat	*Fagopyrum esculentum*
Broad-leaved dock	*Rumex obtusifolius*
Curled dock	*R. crispus*
Common sorrel	*R. acetosa*
Sheep's sorrel	*R. acetosella*
Purple spurge	*Euphorbia peplis*
Sun spurge, or Wolf's milk	*E. helioscopa*
Portland spurge	*E. portlandica*
Petty spurge	*E. peplus*
Wych elm	*Ulmus glabra*
Great nettle	*Urtica dioica*
Small nettle	*U. urens*
Silver birch	*Betula verrucosa*
Common alder	*Alnus glutinosa*
British oak	*Quercus robur*
Turkey oak	*Q. cerris*
Sweet chestnut	*Castanea sativa*
Common beech	*Fagus sylvatica*
Crack willow	*Salix fragilis*
White willow	*S. alba*
Common osier	*S. viminalis*
Auricled sallow	*S. aurita*
Great sallow	*S. caprea*
Common sallow	*S. atrocineraria*
Dwarf willow	*S. repens*
Dark-leaved sallow	*S. nigricans*
Small tree willow	*S. arbuscula*
White poplar	*Populus alba*
Black poplar	*P. nigra*

Autumn lady's tresses	*Spiranthes spiralis*
Early purple orchis	*Orchis mascula*
Marsh orchis	*O. praetermissa*
Heath spotted orchis	*O. ericetorum*
Yellow flag	*Iris pseudacorus*
Common daffodil	*Narcissus pseudo-narcissus*
Pale twin narcissus	*N. biflorus*
Pheasant eye	*N. poeticus*
Bluebell	*Endymian non-scriptus*
Bluebell, var.	*E. n-s. var. longibracteatus*
Bog asphodel	*Narthecium umbellatum*
Toad rush	*Juncus bufonius*
Soft rush	*J. effusus*
Common rush	*J. conglomeratus*
Lesser jointed rush	*J. bulbosus*
Shining-fruited jointed rush	*J. articulatus*
Shining-fruited jointed rush, var.	*J. a. nigritellus*
Sharp-flowered jointed rush	*J. acutiflorus*
Sharp-flowered jointed rush	*J. a. multiflorus*
Many-headed wood-rush	*Luzula multiflora*
Many-headed wood-rush, var.	*L. m. var. congesta*
Cuckoo-pint	*Arum maculatum*
Lesser duck-weed.	*Lemna minor*
? Common star-fruit	*Damasonium alisma*
Oblong-leaved pond-weed	*Potamogeton polygonifolius*
Horned pond-weed	*Zannichellia palustris*
Marsh spike-rush	*Eleocharis palustris*
Many-stemmed spike-rush	*E. multicaulis*
Deer's-hair club-rush	*Trichophorum caespitosum*
Floating club-rush	*Eleogiton fluitans*
Bristle-like club-rush	*Isolepis setacea*
Narrow-leaved cotton-grass	*Eriophorum angustifolium*
Flea sedge	*Carex pulicaris*
Sand sedge	*C. arenaria*
Great-panicled sedge	*C. paniculata*
Star-headed sedge	*C. echinata*
Common tufted sedge	*C. nigra*
Glaucous sedge	*C. flacca*
Carnation-leaved sedge	*C. panicea*
Smooth-stalked sedge	*C. laevigata*
Yellow sedge	*C. serotina*
Bottle sedge	*C. spicata*

L

Oval sedge	*C. ovalis*
Oval sedge, var.	*C. o. var. flava*
Sweet-scented vernal grass	*Anthoxanthum odoratum*
Marsh fox-tail grass	*Alopecurus geniculatus*
Common timothy-grass	*Phleum pratense*
Brown bent-grass	*Agrostis canina*
Fine bent-grass	*A. tenuis*
Black bent-grass	*A. gigantea*
White bent-grass	*A. stolonifera*
Silvery hair-grass	*Aira caryophyllea*
Early hair-grass	*A. praecox*
Tufted hair-grass	*Deschampsia caespitosa*
Wavy hair-grass	*D. flexuosa*
Yorkshire fog	*Holcus lanatus*
Common flase cat	*Arrhenatherum elatius*
Decumbent heath grass	*Sieglingia decumbens*
Crested dog's-tail grass	*Cynosurus cristatus*
Purple melic grass	*Molinia caerulea*
Cock's-foot grass	*Dactylis glomerata*
Annual meadow grass	*Poa annua*
Flat-stemmed meadow grass	*P. compressa*
Rough meadow grass	*P. trivialis*
Dwarf darnel-like manna grass	*Desmazeria marina*
Squirrel's-tail-fescue or Barren fescue	*Vulpia bromoides*
Sheep's fescue	*Festuca ovina*
Barren brome	*Bromus sterilis*
Rye-brome	*B. secalinus*
Rye-brome, var.	*B. s. var. velutinus*
Soft brome	*Bromus vudlis*
Slender false brome	*Brachypodium sylvaticum*
Rye grass	*Lolitum perenne*
Italian rye grass	*L. multiflorum*
Couch grass	*Agropyron repens*
Mat grass	*Nardus stricta*
Scots pine	*Pinus sylvestris*

Ferns:

Maiden-hair fern	*Adiantum capillus-veneris*
Bracken	*Pteridium aquilinum*
Hard fern	*Blechnum spicant*
Lanceolate spleenwort	*Asplenium obovatum*

Black spleenwort	*A. adiantum-nigrum*
Black spleenwort, var.	*A. a-n. var. obtusum*
Sea spleenwort	*A. marinum*
Black maiden-hair spleenwort	*A. trichomanes*
Lady fern	*Athyrium filix-femina*
Hart's tongue	*Phyllitis scolopendrium*
Brittle bladder fern	*Cystopteris fragilis*
Prickly shield fern	*Polystichum aculeatum*
Male fern	*Dryopteris filix-mas*
Male fern, var.	*D. f-m. pumila*
Narrow buckler-fern	*D. spinulosa*
Broad buckler-fern	*D. austriaca*
Hay-scented buckler-fern	*D. aemula*
Common polypody	*Polypodium vulgare*
Royal fern	*Osmunda regalis*
Adder's tongue	*Ophioglossum vulgatum*
Adder's tongue, var.	*O. p. polyphyllum*
Moonwort	*Botrychium lunaria*

APPENDIX I

The Fauna of Lundy

BIRDS

1 BLACK-THROATED DIVER, *Colymbus articus*.
Three records, single birds November 1951, April 1964, Spring 1967.

2 GREAT NORTHERN DIVER, *Colymbus immer*.
Rare visitor. Recorded 1860, 1874 (doubtful), 1927(2), 1944, 1951, 1952, and annually from 1956 to 1962. 1966.

4 RED-THROATED DIVER, *Colymbus stellatus*.
Irregular visitor. Spring, or more rarely autumn passage. Recorded: September 1926, April 1939, October 1941, May 1947, 1951, 1952, 1953 (two birds during March), 1955, 1956, 1957, 1962, 1963.

6 RED-NECKED GREBE, *Podiceps griseigena*.
First record single bird, August 1957.

7 SLAVONIAN GREBE, *Podiceps auritus*.
Four birds present April 1947; single birds November 1951, October 1955, March 1957.

8 BLACK-NECKED GREBE, Podiceps caspicus.
Rare visitor. Single birds April 1947 and November 1951. 'One in the Ilfracombe Museum was shot on Lundy many years ago'.

9 LITTLE GREBE, *Podicpes ruficollis*.
Rare visitor. Recorded October 1949, April 1963, August 1964.

12 LEACH'S FORK-TAILED PETREL, *Oceonodroma leucorrhoa*.
One dead bird found June 1928.

14 STORM PETREL, *Hydrobates pelagicus*.
Irregular visitor. Recorded 1933, 1948, 1962. Ten seen offshore April 1950. Several hundreds seen north of the island July 1953. Dead birds found 1954, 1956, 1959, 1961 and 1962.

16 MANX SHEARWATER, *Procellaria puffinus*.
Breeds in small numbers, not always successfully probably due to rats. Considerable summer visitors.

— BALEARIC SHEARWATER, *P. p. mauretanicus.*
Two seen offshore September 1950. Single near Rat Island, July 1959.

19 GREAT SHEARWATER, *Procellaria gravis.*
Very rare. Three records, two birds in each case; April 1939, April 1950 and offshore September 1950.

26 FULMER PETREL, *Fulmarus glacialis.*
Has bred since 1944 in small but increasing numbers. First visit 1921. Eight chicks reared in 1955, 13 in 1956, 16 in 1958; 35 bred in 1959 but 32 pairs in 1962. 27 pairs in 1965.

27 GANNET, *Sula bassana.*
Numbers declined after mid-nineteenth century due to persecution. Final colony on the NW point displaced when North Light built. There had been 16 nests in 1887, 70 pairs bred in 1889 and 30 pairs bred in 1893. No young had been reared on Gannet's Rock since 1883 but at this time there were still 15 pairs nesting there. In 1900, three pairs were breeding at the NW point but no young were reared. In 1901, seven pairs nested. The five pairs nesting in 1903 in a cove below the lighthouse laid five eggs, but all of these were taken.
This is the last Lundy record and from this time dates the establishment of the now large colony on Grassholm. One pair made strenuous efforts to return in 1922 but there was thick fog at the time and they were driven away by the North Light foghorn.
Gannets are still frequently seen flying close offshore, fifty being seen together in August 1961 and 100+ off the Battery August 1966.

28 CORMORANT, *Phalacrocorax carbo.*
Resident : 1–4 pairs bred until mid 1960s. Small spring and autumn passage.

29 SHAG, *Phalacrocorax aristotelis.*
Resident. Breeding population 1956 132 pairs. 1965 53 pairs.

30 HERON, *Ardea cinerea.*
Annual visitor, mostly between June and September; usually single birds, but three recorded 1956, 1957 and 1958; and four in 1965.

32 LITTLE EGRET, *Egretta garzetta.*
First record, one June 1957, male, died. Now stuffed and preserved in Marisco tavern.

38 BITTERN, *Botaurus stellaris.*
Chanter lists as 'occasional visitor'. Only recent record one exhausted bird found September 1930.

43 GLOSSY IBIS, *Plegadis falcinellus.*
Listed by Chanter as an 'occasional visitor'.

45 MALLARD, *Anas platyrhyncha.*
Rare visitor. Single birds recorded 1951, 1952, 1954 and 1957. Three pairs nested near the Punchbowl, 1921. Pair introduced 1958, 4 or 5 pairs bred 1959, 1962, 1967.

46 TEAL, *Anas crecca.*
Frequent visitor mostly in autumn and winter, numbers usually 1–4. Maximum of 9 in December 1959.

47 GARGENY, *Anas querquedula.*
First record, single bird 1958. Three seen March 1959.

49 GADWALL, *Anas strepera.*
One bird July 1947; one pair April and two drakes, May 1952.

50 WIDGEON, *Anas penelope.*
Autumn and winter visitor, small numbers.

52 PINTAIL DUCK, *Anas acuta.*
Single birds, December 1932, September 1964.

53 SHOVELER, *Spatula clypeata.*
Four records : November 1904 (one shot), March-April 1929 (pair), March-April 1949 (one), July-August 1967.

55 SCAUP, *Aythya marila.*
First record, single bird in oiled condition 9 October 1955 (found dead following day). Female 5 October 1965.

56 TUFTED DUCK, *Aythya fuligula.*
Five records, all single birds : April 1938, October 1941, October 1943, April 1963, March 1966.

57 POCHARD, *Aythya ferina.*
Two records, single birds : April 1939, February 1954.

60 GOLDENEYE, *Bucephala clangula.*
One record, single bird : October 1941.

63 SURF SCOTER, *Melanitta perspicillata.*
First record, single bird 1956.

64 COMMON SCOTER, *Melanitta nigra.*
Irregular visitor. Single birds 1948, 1949, 1950, 1951; April-May 1955 (two birds), singles 1956 and 1959.

69 RED-BREASTED MERGANSER, *Mergus serrator.*
Single bird December 1938.

70 GOOSANDER, *Mergus merganser.*
Single bird December 1934.

71 SMEW, *Mergus albellus.*
Single bird September 1933.

73 SHELDUCK, *Tadorna tadorna.*
Only two records, January 1881, 28-30th August 1966.

74 RUDDY SHELDUCK, *Casarca ferruginea.*
Only record, single bird September 1944.

75 GREYLAG GOOSE, *Anser anser.*
One caught September 1949, another seen April-May 1964.

76 WHITE-FRONTED GOOSE, *Anser albifrons.*
Rare visitor. Seven identified between 1877 and 1880.
Recorded : 1938 (one), 1939 (two), 1949 (eight in October).
One was present with the tame geese January-March 1953
and again in February 1955.

— BEAN GOOSE, *Anser arvensis.*
Rare visitor. Recorded 1860–1 (small flock), December 1932
(nine), October 1935 (ten), March-April 1940 (one).

— PINK-FOOTED GOOSE, *Anser brachyrhynchus.*
Recorded January 1940 (two) and singles December 1949
and October 1959.

80 BRENT GOOSE, *Branta bernicula.*
Single birds recorded January 1933, April 1940, September
1947.

81 BARNACLE GOOSE, *Branta leucopsis.*
Recorded April-May 1941 (one), September 1944 (three),
April 1959 (one), October-November 1966 (six).

82 CANADA GOOSE, *Branta canadensis.*
One shot about 1914.

84 MUTE SWAN, *Cygnus olor.*
One on water 400 yd off Jenny's Cove 10 September 1959.

85 WHOOPER SWAN, *Cygnus cygnus.*
Six present November 1949; two present November 1962.

89 GOLDEN EAGLE, *Aquila chrysaetus.*
Chanter lists as occasional visitor, but probably mistaken.

90 SPOTTED EAGLE, *Aquila clanga.*
One possibly, shot and lost 1858.

91 BUZZARD, *Buteo buteo.*
Bred until 1958. Unsuccessful pair 1959, 1962, 1963, 1965.

92 ROUGH-LEGGED BUZZARD, *Buteo lagopus.*
First record, single bird November 1959.

93 SPARROW HAWK, *Accipiter nisus.*
One pair bred in 1922. Recorded annually on spring and autumn passage, usually single birds.

94 GOSHAWK, *Accipiter gentilis.*
First record, single bird April 1951.

95 KITE, *Milvus milvus.*
Chanter lists as occasional visitor. Three birds seen in flight over the island in April 1929.

97 WHITE-TAILED EAGLE, *Haliaetus albicilla.*
One bird shot about 1880. Formerly bred.

99 MARSH HARRIER, *Circus aeruginosus.*
Rare visitor. Recorded October 1944 (two birds), singles November 1944 and in 1958.

100 HEN HARRIER, *Circus cyaneus.*
Rare visitor. Recorded 1860–1, 1934, 1937 (two), 1951, 1958, 1963, 1964, 1966, 1967.

102 MONTAGU'S HARRIER, *Circuspygargus.*
Rare visitor. Recorded single birds 1937, 1948, 1950, 1958, 1960, 1961 and 1962.

103 OSPREY, *Pandion Haliaetus.*
One pair nested regularly near Gannets Bay until 1838 when the mate was shot.

104 HOBBY, *Falco subbuteo.*
Rare visitor. Recorded March 1936, March 1948 (two birds), September 1950, September 1959, August 1960, April 1962, May 1964, 1965, 1966, 1967.

105 PEREGRINE FALCON, *Falco peregrinus.*
Breeds irregularly, not always successfully. Young were reared by one pair in 1950, 1953 and 1955.

— GREENLAND FALCON, *Falco rusticolus candicans.*
Recorded three times : mid-nineteenth century, 1903 and 1937.

107 MERLIN, *Falco columbarius.*
Spring and autumn passage, usually one or two birds.

110 KESTREL, *Falco tinnunculus.*
Breeds irregularly, one or two pairs bred annually 1950–4, 1956–9, 1962 and 3. Spring and autumn passage, small numbers.

111 RED GROUSE, *Lagopus scoticus.*
Various attempts to introduce this bird have been unsuccessful.

116 PARTRIDGE, *Perdix perdix.*

An unsuccessful attempt at introduction was made in the late nineteenth century, again in 1928, and in 1966.

117 QUAIL, *Coturnix coturnix.*
Once bred; 13 or 14 nests were found in 1870. Only recent records: June 1937 (pair), June 1948 (probable) and May 1953 (dead bird). At least one bird present in 1958, 1964, 1965 and 1967.

118 PHEASANT, *Phasianus colchicus.*
Introduced about 1880 and again, successfully, about 1920. Two or three pairs have bred annually since 1922. Maximum of 12 birds recorded in 1957.

120 WATER-RAIL, *Rallus aquaticus.*
Spring and autumn passage, small numbers. Also some winter residents.

121 SPOTTED CRAKE, *Porzana porzana.*
Dated records single bird May 1887, probable August 1966, definite May 1967.

124 LITTLE CRAKE, *Porzana parva.*
Only dated record one bird September 1952.

125 CORNCRAKE, *Crex crex.*
Spring and autumn passage, usually only one or two birds. Formerly bred, last occasion probably 1935.

126 MOORHEN, *Gallinula chloropus.*
Rare visitor. Recorded 1931, February 1936, June 1950, December 1951, February 1952, April 1955, May 1964, 1966, 1967.

127 COOT, *Fulica atra.*
Rare visitor. Recorded December 1927 and early January 1928, December 1932, January 1933, March 1939, March and October 1941, December 1951, October 1957, 1966.

131 OYSTERCATCHER, *Haematopus ostralegus.*
Present throughout the year; 1961 breeding population of 18 pairs, but only 8–10 pairs in 1963 and 1965, 17 pairs bred in 1967.

133 LAPWING, *Vanellus vanellus.*
Resident, breeding population (1967) of 20 pairs increasing. Also spring and autumn passage in considerable numbers, and winter visitor.

134 RINGED PLOVER, *Charadrius hiaticula.*
Spring and autumn passage, small numbers.

139 GREY PLOVER, *Charadrius squatarola.*
Occasional visitor. Recorded 1928, 1930, 1938 (40–50 birds),

October 1938, 1939 (24 birds), 1953, 1957, 1959, 1963, 1966.

140 GOLDEN PLOVER, *Charadrius apricaria.*
Regular spring and autumn passage, small numbers; also occasional winter visitor.

142 DOTTEREL, *Charadrius morinellus.*
Visitor. Recorded 1937, 1942, 1947, 1949 (eight), 1951, 1956 (two), 1959, 1960 (two), 1961 (five), 1962, 1966 (five), 1967.

143 TURNSTONE, *Arenaria interpres.*
Spring and autumn passage, small numbers.

145 SNIPE, *Capella gallinago.*
Recorded all months and on spring and autumn passage. Believed to have bred rarely.

GREAT SNIPE, *Capella media.*
No dated records, one killed on Lundy in the nineteenth century and listed by Chanter as 'autumn and winter visitor'.

147 JACK SNIPE, *Lymnocryptes minimus.*
Recorded almost annually in small numbers on spring and autumn passage and in the winter.

148 WOODCOCK, *Scoloplax rusticola.*
Autumn and winter visitor, small numbers, almost annually.

150 CURLEW, *Numenius arquata.*
Resident, breeds irregularly probably only one pair. Common on spring passage, less so on autumn passage.

151 WHIMBREL, *Numenius phaeopus.*
Regular spring and autumn passage, moderate numbers.

154 BLACK-TAILED GODWIT, *Limosa limosa.*
Rare visitor. Recorded 1938, 1939, 1940, 1943, 1952, 1956, 1957, 1959, 1963, 1967.

155 BAR-TAILED GODWIT, *Limosa lapponica.*
Rare visitor. Recorded 1933 (two or three), 1936, 1938, 1948, 1949, 1958, 1959 (two), 1962, 1965.

156 GREEN SANDPIPER, *Tringa ocrophus.*
Irregular spring and autumn passage single birds June 1930, May 1931, August 1932, May 1938 (two birds), September 1951, August 1952, August 1953, April 1954, August 1956, September 1958, September 1962, May 1964, 1965, 1967.

157 WOOD SANDPIPER, *Tringa glareola.* August 1967.

159 COMMON SANDPIPER, *Tringa hypoleucos.*
Regular spring and autumn passage, small numbers.

161 REDSHANK, *Tringa totanus.*
Regular spring and autumn passage, small numbers.

162 SPOTTED REDSHANK, *Tringa erythropus.*
Six records : March 1954, August 1955, August 1959 (two birds) August 1962, August 1966 (three), August 1967.

163 LESSER YELLOWLEGS, *Tringa flavipes.*
First record, single bird October 1959.

165 GREENSHANK, *Tringa nebularia.*
Visitor. Recorded September 1947, 1950, 1952 and annually 1954–1967.

169 KNOT, *Calidris canutus.*
Rare visitor. Recorded 1952, 1956, 1959, 1960, 1961, 1962, 1964, 1967.

170 PURPLE SANDPIPER, *Calidris maritima.*
Occasional visitor. Recorded winter 1928 (4 birds), January 1931, May (4 birds) and September 1949, September 1951, December 1954, April 1955 (2 birds), October 1956 (dead), October 1959, August 1962, May 1964, November 1967.

171 LITTLE STINT, *Calidris minuta.*
Rare visitor. Recorded 1956, September 1957 (8 birds), September 1960 (3 birds), October 1962, October 1964, 1966, 1967.

172 AMERICAN STINT, *Calidris minutilla.*
First record, single bird September 1957. Again 8 September 1966 and 14 September 1966.

176 PECTORAL SANDPIPER, *Calidris melanotos.*
Rare visitor. Recorded October 1950, October 1960, August 1961, September 1962, September 1967.

178 DUNLIN, *Calidris alpina. (C. a. schinzii and C. a. alpina).*
Regular spring and autumn passage, small numbers.

179 CURLEW SANDPIPER, *Calidris testacea.*
Rare visitor. Recorded September 1927, May 1939, September 1958, May 1959, September 1967.

180 SEMI-PALMATED SANDPIPER, *Calidris Pusilla.*
First Lundy record 8 September 1966, trapped and ringed.

181 SANDERLING, *Crocethia alba.*
Irregular visitor in autumn. One spring record only May 1934. Recorded 1948, 1950, 1951, 1952, 1954, 1955, 1960, 1961, 1964.

182 BUFF-BREASTED SANDPIPER, *Tryngites subruficollis.*
First record, one shot autumn 1858, now in Taunton Castle

187

museum. One caught September 1959 St Helen's field. 2 birds 27 September 1965.

184 RUFF, *Philomachus pugnax.*
Recent records : September 1937, August 1956, September 1958 (4 male and 5 female birds), August-September 1962, April 1963, 1965, 1967.

187 GREY PHALAROPE, *Phalaroups fulicarius.*
Rare visitor. Recorded December 1881 (shot), September 1941, October 1943, September 1948, September 1951, October 1959, September 1960 (two), probable 1965.

188 RED-NECKED PHALAROPE, *Phalaropus lobatus.*
Two records only : November 1955, October 1960, both single birds.

189 STONE CURLEW, *Burhinus oedicnemus.*
Three records, all single birds : March 1938, May and October 1939.

190 PRATINCOLE, *Glareola pratincola.*
First record, single bird February-March 1945, and possible second visitor April 1962.

193 ARCTIC SKUA, *Stercorarius parasiticus.*
Irregular summer visitor. Recorded September 1947, August 1948, September 1949, September 1953 (two birds in each case), April 1963, 1966.

194 GREAT SKUA, *Stercorarius skua.*
Only record, single bird August 1948.

196 LONG-TAILED SKUA, *Stercorarius longicaudus.*
Only record, single bird seen between Lundy and the mainland, September 1942.

198 GREAT BLACK-BACKED GULL, *Larus marinus.*
Resident, breeds, seen in all months. Present breeding population about 49 pairs, increasing.

199 LESSER BLACK-BACKED GULL, *Larus fascus.*
Resident, breeds. Also spring and autumn passage. Breeding population declined from 350 pairs in 1939 to 55 pairs in 1955, but 69 pairs in 1962, 70 pairs in 1965, 45 pairs in 1967.

200 HERRING GULL, *Larus argentatus.*
Resident, breeds, seen all the year round. Breeding population estimated 2,000 pairs 1922, 3,000 pairs 1939 but accurate count in 1962 recorded over 1,000 pairs, 1,608 nests in 1967.

201 COMMON GULL, *Larus canus.*
Occasional visitor between August and March, small numbers. Recent records 1951, 1952, 1955, 1956, 1958, 1959, 1962, 1965, 1967.

203 ICELAND GULL, *Larus glaucoides.*
Rare visitor. Three certain records; April 1939, April 1950 and November 1952. Records for April 1949 and March 1952 uncertain whether of Iceland Gull or Glaucous Gull *(Larus hyperboreus).*

207 LITTLE GULL, *Larus minutus.*
Two records, October 1891, September 1948.

208 BLACK-HEADED GULL, *Larus ridibundus.*
Seen all year, most common June-July and September-October. Usually small numbers.

209 SABINE'S GULL, *Xema sabini.*
First record, September 1958.

211 KITTIWAKE, *Rissa tridactyla.*
Resident, breeds. Not seen during winter. Breeding population 1,858 pairs in 1953, 250 pairs May 1961, 760 pairs 1962, 1,256 nests 1967.

212 BLACK TERN, *Chlidonias Niger.*
One seen Landing Bay August 1967.

217 COMMON TERN, *Sterna hirundo* and
281 ARCTIC TERN, *Sterna paradisea.*
Seen almost annually on autumn passage, small numbers. Only spring records, April 1948 and May 1962.

222 LITTLE TERN, *Sterna albifrons.*
Rare visitor. Recorded May 1939, September 1950 and September 1955.

223 SANDWICH TERN, *Sterna sandvicensis.*
Recorded April 10 1950 (one), April 11 (two), September 1953, (one), September 1959 (seven), 1965.

224 RAZORBILL, *Alca torda.*
Present February to July. Breeds in large numbers, 10,500 pairs in 1939 but only 2,130 individuals in 1962. 1,602 birds 1967.

225 GREAT AUK, *Alba impennis.*
Extinct since 1844. One supposed to have been picked up dead in 1829 and an egg found in 1838 or 1839 was thought to have been an egg of this bird, whom residents described as having been present in recent years.

226   LITTLE AUK, *Plautus alle*.
Only recent records, September 1926, June 1950 (dead), November 1958 (two birds).

227   GUILLEMOT, *Uria aalge*.
Spring and summer resident, breeds. Breeding population estimated at about 5,000 pairs in 1951, but only 3,560 individuals in 1962. One bird caught in November 1951 was of the Northern variety, *U. a. aalge*. 2,355 birds 1967.

230   PUFFIN, *Fratercula artica*.
Summer resident, breeds. Number of breeding birds is declining, probably due to rats : 3,500 pairs in 1939, 400 pairs in 1952, 150 pairs in 1958, 93 pairs in 1962, 33 pairs in 1965, 110 birds 1967.

231   PALLAS'S SAND-GROUSE, *Syrrhaptes paradoxus*.
A flock of seven birds was present in the irruption of 1888.

232   STOCK DOVE, *Columba oenas*.
Irregular spring and autumn passage, very small numbers. Recorded September 1926, March 1949, May 1951, March, April and November 1952, spring and autumn 1953, April and October (eight birds), 1955, October 1956, October 1958, November 1959, September 1963, August 1964, 1965, 1967.

233   ROCK DOVE, *Columba livia*.
Probably bred formerly. Only recent records May and October 1947.

234   WOOD PIGEON, *Columba palumbus*.
Resident, breeds in small numbers. Some spring and autumn passage. 50 seen August 1967.

235   TURTLE DOVE, *Streptopelia turtur*.
Regular spring and autumn passage, moderate numbers. Possibly bred formerly.

COLLARED DOVE, *Streptopelia decaocto*.
First Lundy and Devon record May 1961. Two birds in May 1963. Five May-July 1965, thirteen May 1966, six May 1967.

237   CUCKOO, *Cuculus canorus*.
Breeds irregularly, 1 to 4 pairs. Spring and autumn passage.

239   YELLOW-BILLED CUCKOO, *Coccyzus americanus*.
One picked up dead at Old Light October 1874.

240   BLACK-BILLED CUCKOO, *Coccyzus erythrophthalmus*.
First Lundy record female seen 19 October 1967. Found dead following day.

241 BARN OWL, *Tyto alba.*
Rare visitor. Recorded between 1871 and 1911. (M.C.H.H.);
From July 1922 1 pair were present for a year; single birds
seen 1928, 1932, 1936, 1939, 1957.

246 LITTLE OWL, *Athene noctua.*
Rare visitor. Three records, all single birds, June 1933,
November 1944, June 1955.

247 TAWNY OWL, *Strix aluco.*
Recorded October 1957 and April 1958.

248 LONG-EARED OWL, *Asio otus.*
One caught January 1930, singles seen October 15th 1954.
May 1962, 1966, 1967.

249 SHORT-EARED OWL, *Asio flammeus.*
Spring and autumn passage, sometimes present in winter.
Recorded annually from 1950.

252 NIGHTJAR, *Caprimulgus europaeus.*
Recorded most years on spring and autumn passage, usually
only one or two birds. No definite evidence of breeding.

255 SWIFT, *Apus apus.*
Spring and autumn passage, numbers variable; sometimes
seen in the summer.

257 ALPINE SWIFT, *Apus melba.*
Three records of single birds : May 1959, April 1962, September 1965.

258 KINGFISHER, *Alcedo atthis.*
Irregular visitor. Single birds recorded 1947, 1952, 1953,
1957, 1960, 1961.

259 BEE-EATER, *Merops apiaster.*
Six birds present for one week May 1940.

260 ROLLER, *Coracias garrulus.*
First record, single bird August 1949.

261 HOOPOE, *Upupa epops.*
Seen irregularly on spring migration; recorded 1923 (five
birds), 1941, 1943, 1950–55, 1957–59, 1961–3, 1965, 1966.
Also five autumn records of single birds 1949, 1958, 1959,
1962, and 1967.

263 GREAT SPOTTED WOODPECKER, *Dendrocopus major.*
Records single birds : October 1949, September 1957, August-September 1959, September 1964, October 1962 (two),
1965, 1967.

265 WRYNECK, *Jynx torquilla.*

191

Single birds recorded May and September 1949, April and September 1956, 1959, 1960, 1963, 1967.

— BIMACULATED LARK, *Melamocorypha bimaculata.*
First record in Britain, single bird at Benjamin's Chair, 7 May 1962.

271 WOODLARK, *Lullula arborea.*
Single birds in spring or autumn, first recorded 1950 and annually since then.

272 SKYLARK, *Alauda arvensis.*
Resident, breeds (about 40 pairs 1967). Light spring and heavier autumn passage.

273 SHORE LARK, *Eremophila alpestris.*
Very rare visitor. Only recent record, single bird March 1944.

274 SWALLOW, *Hirundo rustica.*
Large numbers on spring and autumn passage (500 seen 17 May 1963 and 1,000 seen 11 September 1964). Occasionally breeds, one pair 1952, 1959, 1962 and 1963, one pair bred 1967.

275 RED-RUMPED SWALLOW, *Hirundo daurica.*
First record, single bird 27 March 1952.

276 HOUSE MARTIN, *Delichon urbica.*
Spring and autumn passage, numbers variable.

277 SAND MARTIN, *Riparia riparia.*
Large numbers spring and autumn passage.

278 GOLDEN ORIOLE, *Oriolus oriolus.*
Occasional spring visitor. Recorded 1947, 1949, 1951, 1952, 1953, 1955, 1957, 1958, 1959, 1965, 1967 (five).

— BALTIMORE ORIOLE, *Icterus galbula.*
First British record, single birds female. 2 October 1958. Two seen 17 October 1967.

279 RAVEN, *Corvus corax.*
Resident. In recent years 1–4 pairs have bred, or attempted to breed. 9 breeding pairs 1966.

280 CARRION CROW, *Corvus corone.*
Resident, 1 to 8 breeding pairs. Spring and autumn passage, maximum autumn numbers 60.

281 HOODED CROW, *Corvus cornix.*
Seven records of single birds : 1948, 1949, 1952, 1953, 1958, 1962, 1964.

282 ROOK, *Corvus frugilegus.*
Spring passage. Usually 1–2, but maximum of 12 in 1953.

283 JACKDAW, *Corvus monedula.*
Spring, and more rarely autumn passage. Small numbers.
Six residents March-April 1956.

284 MAGPIE, *Pica pica.*
Irregular visitor. Recorded 1887–8, 1930–32, 1934, 1938,
1939, 1946, 1952, 1953.

286 JAY, *Garrulus Glandarius.*
First Lundy record, single bird 26 September 1965.

287 CHOUGH, *Coracia pyrrhocorrax.*
Numerous until late nineteenth century. Formerly bred.
Only recent records are single birds October 1949 and
February 1952.

288 GREAT TIT, *Parus major.*
First record, single bird wintered 1939–40. Annually since
1949 spring and autumn passage, only 1–4 birds. One bird
wintered on the island 1952–3; 10–15 seen daily October
1957.

289 BLUE TIT, *Parus caeruleus.*
Irregular visitor. Recorded 1932, 1943, 1944, 1949, 1951,
1952, 1954, 1957, 1959, 1962. Usually single birds but
maximum 80 in October 1957.

290 COAL TIT, *Parus ater.*
Irregular visitor. Recorded 1932, 1943, 1944, 1949, 1950,
1954, 1955, 1957, 1959, 1966, 1967. Usually 1–2 birds spring
or autumn, but about 30 in October 1957.

292 MARSH TIT, *Parus palustris.*
First record, single bird January 1958.

294 LONG-TAILED TIT, *Aegithalos caudatus.*
Rare visitor : 5–8 birds recorded autumn 1932, 1944, 1952
and 1–2 birds October 1954; 6 in October 1957; 12 in
October 1958; 1 in 1960.

298 TREE CREEPER, *Certhia familiaris.*
Recorded 1950, 1953, 1956–60, 1966, 1967, all single
birds.

299 WREN, *Troglodytes troglodytes.*
Resident, breeds. Six pairs bred 1967.

301 MISTLE THRUSH, *Turdus viscivorus.*
Spring and autumn passage, small numbers; 20 seen November 1958. Formerly bred 1929–41 (one pair).

302 FIELDFARE, *Turdus pilaris.*
Spring and autumn passage, considerable numbers. Also
recorded in winter.

M

303   SONG THRUSH, *Turdus ericetorum.*
Spring and autumn passage, variable numbers. Breeds spasmodically, maximum of 9 pairs 1930.

—   CONTINENTAL SONG THRUSH, *T. e philomelus.*
One bird trapped November 1951, thought to have been of this type.

304   REDWING, *Turdus musicus.*
Spring and autumn passage, large numbers.

—   ICELANDIC REDWING, *T. m. coburni.*
One bird trapped November 1951.

307   RING-OUSEL, *Turdus torquatus.*
Spring and autumn passage, small numbers.

308   BLACKBIRD, *Turdus merula.*
Some birds present all year, breeding population now about 15 pairs. Considerable numbers on spring and autumn passage.

309   WHITE'S THRUSH, *Turdus dauma.*
First definite record, October 1952, single bird.

—   AMERICAN ROBIN, *Turdus migratorium.*
First record for Lundy and Britain, single bird present 27 October to 8 November 1952. Second record 7 November 1962.

311   WHEATEAR, *Oenanthe oenanthe.*
Breeding population now 3–10 pairs. Considerable numbers on spring and autumn passage.

317   STONECHAT, *Saxicola torquata.*
Bred regularly in numbers up to 28 pairs until 1942; one pair bred 1951–3; 4 pairs possibly bred 1960; at least six pairs bred 1962. Regular spring and autumn passage, usually small numbers, some birds present in winter.

318   WHINCHAT, *Saxicola rubetra.*
Spring and autumn passage, usually small numbers.

320   REDSTART, *Phoenicurus phoenicurus.*
Regular spring and autumn passage, small numbers.

321   BLACK REDSTART, *Phoenicurus ochrurus.*
Spring and autumn passage, small numbers.

322   NIGHTINGALE, *Luscinia megarhynchos.*
Single birds August 1957, August 1961 and April 1963; 1966; 1967.

324   BLUETHROAT, *Cyanosylvia svecica.*
First record for Lundy, September and October 1949, one September 1956, one probable 1960.

325 ROBIN, *Erithacus rubecula.*
Breeding population now 2–10 pairs. Present throughout the year, and on spring and autumn passage.
327 GRASSHOPPER WARBLER, *Locustella naevia.*
Regular spring and autumn passage, small numbers.
331 MOUSTACHED WARBLER, *Luscinicla melanopogon.*
First Lundy record 2 May 1959.
333 REED WARBLER, *Acrocephalus scirpaceus.*
Spring and autumn passage. First recorded 1944, and annually since 1948, usually single birds.
334 MARSH WARBLER, *Acrocephalus palustris.*
One caught and ringed 2 September 1962. One caught 12 September 1967.
337 SEDGE WARBLER, *Acrocephalus schoenobaenus.*
Spring and autumn passage, numbers variable. One pair bred in 1934 and 1935.
338 AQUATIC WARBLER, *Acrocephalus paludicola.*
Two seen 15 September 1949, single August 1956, single May and September 1963.
339 MELODIOUS WARBLER, *Hippolais polyglotta.*
Single birds recorded July 1951 (trapped), August 1954 (trapped), September 1958, 1959, September 1963, 1967 (two).
340 ICTERINE WARBLER, *Hippolais icterina.*
Recorded autumn 1949 (two single birds), autumn 1951 (four single birds), September 1954, August 1955, September 1960 (three), September 1961, September 1962, September 1963; 1966.
343 BLACKCAP, *Sylvia atricapilla.*
Spring and autumn passage, small numbers.
344 BARBED WARBLER, *Sylvia nisoria.*
First record, single bird October 1949. September 1960 (two), 1966, 1967 (six).
346 GARDEN WARBLER, *Sylvia borin.*
Spring and autumn passage, small numbers.
347 WHITETHROAT, *Sylvia communis.*
Spring and autumn passage, considerable numbers, occasionally breeds.
348 LESSER WHITETHROAT, *Sylvia curruca.*
Spring and autumn passage almost annually, small numbers.
352 DARTFORD WARBLER, *Sylvia undata.*
Single birds 28 October 1951 and March 1963.

354 WILLOW WARBLER, *Phylloscopus trochilus.*
Spring and autumn passage variable numbers. Bred almost annually until 1954.

355 GREENISH WARBLER, *Phylloscopus trochiloides.*
First record November 1958, one or two birds.

356 CHIFFCHAFF, *Phylloscopus collybita.*
Regular spring and autumn passage, numbers variable.
NORTHERN CHIFFCHAFF.
Three autumn records, 1949, 1952, 1955 (two birds).

357 WOOD WARBLER, *Phylloscopus sibilatrix.*
Spring and autumn passage, small numbers. First recorded 1932 and almost annually since 1947.

358 BONELLI'S WARBLER, *Phylloscopus bonelli.*
First record for Lundy and second in Britain, one bird caught 1 September 1954. Two seen August 1960.

359 ARCTIC WARBLER, *Phylloscopus borealis.*
First record, single bird trapped 6 September 1959.

360 YELLOW-BROWED WARBLER, *Phylloscopus inornatus.*
Six records, all single birds: April 1944, October 1949, October 1950, November 1955, October 1962, 1967.

— YELLOWTHROAT, *Geothlypis trichas.*
First record for Lundy and Europe, male caught 4 November 1954.

— MYRTLE WARBLER, *Dendroica coronata.*
First Lundy and second British record, single bird trapped, ringed and photographed, November 1960.

364 GOLDCREST, *Regulus regulus.*
Regular spring and autumn passage, small numbers. Occasionally seen in winter. One pair bred 1922, 1923, 1952.

365 FIRECREST, *Regulus ignicapillus.*
Irregular visitor but recorded almost every year from 1949.

366 SPOTTED FLYCATCHER, *Muscicapa striata.*
Regular spring and autumn passage, fair numbers. One pair bred in 1956, 1957, 1959, 1962, 1963.

368 PIED FLYCATCHER, *Muscicapa hypoleuca.*
Regular spring and autumn passage, numbers variable.

370 RED-BREASTED FLYCATCHER, *Muscicapa parva.*
Recorded 1950, 1951 (two), 1954, 1955, 1957, 1958, 1959, 1962, 1966, 1967 (two).

371 DUNNOCK OR HEDGE SPARROW, *Prunella modularis.*
Resident. Breeding population 1967 7 pairs.

373 MEADOW PIPIT, *Anthus pratensis.*

Resident. Also large numbers spring and autumn passage (640 on 26 September 1964). Breeding population 1965 about 30 birds.

374 RICHARD'S PIPIT, *Anthus richardi.*
First record October 1957, again September and October 1958 and probably September 1960, all single birds. Two from 14–22 September, 1963. Three September 1966. Three 1967.

375 TAWNY PIPIT, *Anthus campestris.*
First record, single bird October 1950. Single birds seen September 1951, November 1966.

376 TREE PIPIT, *Anthus trivialis.*
Spring and autumn passage, small numbers.

378 RED-THROATED PIPIT, *Anthus cervinus.*
First record, pair, 7 May 1959. One caught and ringed.

379 ROCK PIPIT, *Anthus spinoletta.*
Resident breeds. 23 pairs 1967.

380 PIED WAGTAIL, *Motacilla alba.*
Resident, and spring and autumn passage together with White Wagtails. Irregular breeder; 1922–42 (1–6 pairs), 1953 (one pair), 1954 (one pair double brooded), 1956 (one pair), 1957 (two pairs), 1958 (four pairs), 1959, 1962 (five pairs), 1966, 1967.

381 GREY WAGTAIL, *Motacilla cinerea.*
Spring and autumn passage, usually small numbers.

382 YELLOW WAGTAIL, *Motacilla flava.*
Spring and autumn passage, usually small numbers.

— BLUE-HEADED WAGTAIL, *M. f. flava.*
Chanter lists as a 'summer visitant'. Only recent record is of two present in May 1947.

383 WAXWING, *Bombycilla garrulus.*
Listed by Chanter as an occasional visitor, no recent records.

385 LESSER GREY SHRIKE, *Lanius minor.*
Three recent records : September 1958 (probable), September 1961, May 1963, all single birds.

386 WOODCHAT SHRIKE, *Lanius senator.*
Rare visitor. Recent records, 1949, 1952, 1953, 1956, 1957, 1958, 1960, 1964, 1966, 1967, all single birds.

388 RED-BACKED SHRIKE, *Lanius collurio.*
Rare visitor. Recorded July 1870, 1949, 1951, 1957, 1958 (2), 1959 (one trapped), 1963, 1964, 1965.

197

389 STARLING, *Sturnus vulgaris.*
Bred in 1938, 1942, 1943, 1962, 1964, 1966. Spring and autumn passage large numbers. At least 20,000 moved north on 7 November 1959. About 18 pairs bred 1967.

390 ROSE-COLOURED STARLING, *Sturnus roseus.*
'Regular spring visitor' during Rev Mr Heaven's ownership. One dated record, single bird June 1934.

391 HAWFINCH, *Coccothraustes coccothraustes.*
Occasional summer visitor, usually single birds. May have bred in 1927.

392 GREENFINCH, *Chloris chloris.*
Spring and autumn passage, usually small numbers 1–25. Has bred rarely.

393 GOLDFINCH, *Carduelis carduelis.*
Spring and autumn passage, small numbers. Bred in 1959, but this is rare.

394 SISKIN, *Carduelis spinus.*
Rare winter visitor. Recorded 1929, 1949 (at least 25), 1952, 1953, 1959 (flock of 250 seen 25 October), 1960, 1963, 1964, 1966. One pair bred May-August 1952.

395 LINNET, *Carduelis cannabina.*
Resident, breeds and passage migrant. Resident breeding population (1953) about 20 pairs, 2 pairs bred 1967.

396 TWITE, *Carduelis flavirostris.*
Rare visitor. Recorded 1937, October 1952, February 1953, June 1954, May 1957.

397 REDPOLL, *Carduelis flammea.*
Rare visitor. Recorded 1874, 1928, 1936, 1948, 1950, 1952, 1953, 1956, 1957, 1959, 1962, 1964, 1965, 1966, 1967, (two).

400 SERIN, *Serinus canarius.*
Recorded April 1943 (4 birds), July-October 1956 (1), April 1959.

401 BULLFINCH, *Pyrrhula pyrrhula.*
Recorded 1931, 1948, 1950, 1957, 1958, 1959, 1961, 1962, 1965, 1966, 1967.

402 SCARLET GROSBEAK, *Carpodacus erythrinus.*
First record, one caught 10 September 1959. One trapped September 1966. One seen 1967

403 PINE GROSBEAK, *Pinicola enucleator.*
First record, one May 1958.

404 CROSSBILL, *Loxia curvirostra.*

Occasional visitor, usually in the autumn. Recorded 1869, 1927 (irruption year), 1930, 1935, 1949 (3), 1953, (50 maximum), 1956 (10), 1958 (30), 1960 (1), 1962 (25), 1963, 1966 (11).

407 CHAFFINCH, *Fringilla montifringilla.*
Resident, breeds in small numbers, also spring and autumn passage (6,000 seen 26 October 1963) Breeding population 8 pairs in 1967.

408 BRAMBLING, *Fringilla montifringilla.*
Regular spring and autumn passage.

— RUFOUS-SIDED TOWHEE, *Pipilo erythrophthalamus.*
First record for Lundy and Britain, female trapped June 1966.

409 YELLOWHAMMER, *Emberiza citrinella.*
Irregular resident. Passage migrants each year, numbers usually small. Bred 1922 (8 pairs), 1923, 1951 (? 2 pairs).

410 CORN BUNTING, *Emberiza calandra.*
Rare visitor. Recorded 1933, 1940 May and November 1951, May 1954; 1965.

412 BLACK-HEADED BUNTING, *Emberiza melanocephala.*
Chanter describes as an autumn and winter visitor but only recent record is of one female, September 1957.

413 RED-HEADED BUNTING, *Emberiza bruniceps.*
Single birds recorded July 1951, September 1951, August 1952, October 1952, June 1953, September 1956, July 1961, 1962, 1964, 1965, 1966, 1967.

415 CIRL BUNTING, *Emberiza cirlus.*
Irregular visitor. Recorded 1900, 1906, 1948, 1949, 1950, 1951.

416 ORTOLAN BUNTING, *Emberiza hortulana.*
First recorded 1949, thence annually, usually autumn passage and single birds.

420 LITTLE BUNTING, *Emberiza pusilla.*
Only record, two birds October 1951.

421 REED BUNTING, *Emberiza schoeniclus.*
Irregular visitor, usually in winter; 1–4 birds recorded 1948, 1949, 1951, 1952, 1953, 1958, 1959, 1962, 1963, 1965, 1966, 1967.

422 LAPLAND BUNTING, *Calcarius lapponicus.*
First record, 1942. Seen annually since 1948, usually less than ten birds, except 1953 when over 100 were seen. All records in autumn.

423 SNOW BUNTING, *Plectrophenax nivalis.*
Regular spring and autumn passage, numbers usually small, except 1950 (maximum 49).

424 HOUSE SPARROW, *Passer domesticus.*
Formerly bred, now an irregular visitor only. Bred almost annually until 1942 when they were largely destroyed, being farm pests. Recent records 1947, 1950, 1951, 1953, 1956 (3), 1957 (3), 1958 (4), 1959 (2), 1960, 1962, 1965, 1967 (3).

425 TREE SPARROW, *Passer montanus.*
Formerly bred. Recently recorded 1951 (1), 1955 (1), 1958 (12), 1959 (1), 1960 (4), 1961 (6) when one pair bred; 1962 and 1963, two pairs bred. 1967 (2).

MAMMALS

A complete census of mammals was undertaken by the Lundy Field Society in 1953, and a further survey of the rat population was made in 1962. The findings are given below with other recent counts and estimates.

PYGMY SHREW. Present 1953.

BAT. One seen May 1953.

RABBIT. Abundant 1953.

BLACK RAT. Few 1953. More common than Brown in 1962 and distributed evenly over the island. Two brown-grey forms of Black recorded :
    R. r. alexandrinus and
    R. r. frugivorus.

BROWN RAT. Abundant 1953. Near human habitations in 1962.

GREY SEAL. 44 seen together June 1953; 89 counted on 6 September 1956.

FALLOW DEER. 30 in 1929; 2 in 1949; 1 doe 1953. Believed extinct 1955.

JAPANESE DEER. 7 in 1929; 33 in 1949; 64 in 1953; 87 in 1956.

RED DEER. 10 in 1929; 28 in 1949; 11 in 1953; 6 or 7 in 1956. Extinct by 1962.

FERAL GOAT. About 40 in 1953; 46 seen in 1956.

SOAY SHEEP. 1 ram and 7 ewes in 1944; 70 or 80 in 1953.

MOUSE. 'One or two' in 1953.

HORSES. 15, including one stallion in 1965.

At the end of 1956, the numbers of wild goats, wild sheep and deer were reduced by 150, and during the succeeding winters the numbers of these animals have been kept down.

APPENDIX J

Report of Marisco Castle, Lundy

MADE BY CHARLES C. WINMILL, JUNE 1928

(Reproduced by kind permission of the Society for the Protection
of Ancient Buildings. N.B. The report is not reproduced here in full.)

I made a careful survey of the castle and its immediate surround-
ings on June 20, 21 and 22. The main walls of buildings are probably the work of the thirteenth century by William de Marisco, but
I am unable to speak with certainty as I did not find any 'worked'
stone to date the building by.

In a building constructed in roughly-dressed stone, parts rebuilt
with the original stone can give the same appearance as the authentic
work. The parts coloured red on the plan that accompanies this
report would appear to be part of the original building. The part
coloured blue indicates buildings altered or added about 100 years
ago. If the masonry on the angles B and C is examined (ie, viewed
from the south-west) the difficulty of dating the building from the
walling will be apparent.* The parts coloured 'red hatched' are
obviously the most recent and were added to the building as a wind
screen to the inner court.

The original walling outside is built so as to incline inwards. The
only part that I was able to plumb (on the sheltered north-east
angle) has a batter of 10 inches in 18 feet.

. . . I think from comparing the 1776 plan it will be evident that
not much value can be attached to the old plan as to the position
of the walls and enclosures said to exist in 1776. I am of the opinion
that the eighteenth-century drawing is of more value as a statement,
than the plan. It will be seen that the small corner towers are indicated in the view, but the embattlements, the embrasures of which
are now partly walled up, are not indicated.

An examination of the actual building shows that the towers

---

* From information which has come to light since the publication of this
report it is known that the castle was built in 1243.

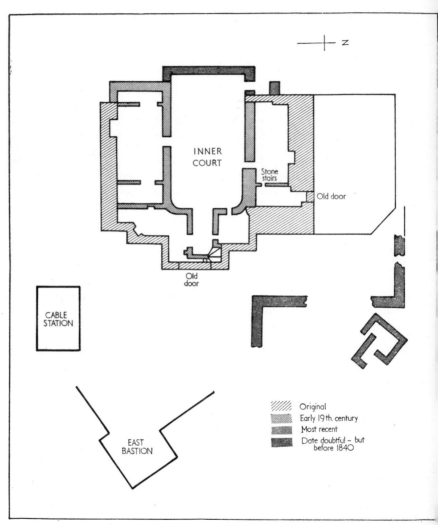

Marisco castle plan showing original building and subsequent additions

which are about five feet in diameter externally, have in recent years been used as chimney stacks, and are not corner bastions, as at first sight one might imagine, and had it not been for the old view might have been taken for modern work, and it is open to question if they were ever used in conjunction with the embattlements for defensive purposes—the embattlements are so indifferently constructed that it is clear (for the greater part) they are sham, ornamental castleated work in vogue at the time of Walpole.

Embattlements and towers may have formed part of the original structure, but the present ones, in character, walling and especially the tabling below the towers at the extreme angles, give one the impression that those existing are not authentic work. . . . I am of the opinion that the angle towers, the embattlements and embrasures, whether built up or not, should remain; that the brick chimney stacks should be removed and that the windows formed in the external walls should be retained with new frames and casements of oak.

Clear the interior of building of all rubbish and remove the parts that are likely to fall. Walling, shown red-hatched, is a wind screen, is badly built and should be pulled down and be rebuilt in the original form.*

Thoroughly repair the outer walls—repoint properly (proper pointing can be seen near the old front door to the hotel).

The mortar should be two parts of washed sea sand, two parts granite dust (as found near Halfway Wall) and one part of Portland cement.

The top of the walling should be repaired, strengthened, and made up to the proper falls and then cemented or asphalted over so as to throw off the rain.

The floor has, I think, been lowered for the cottages and I would suggest that it be brought up to, say, at least the level of the ground outside the castle at the west.

The most permanent way to roof in the castle is to form a steel and concrete flat covering with asphalite at a level of at least 3 feet below the embattlements. This level should be determined by the purpose for which the building will be used. (The mainland cost of such a roof is £230.)

The eastern bastion can be traced and the southern one is probably under the mound of earth at the south, but unless there is some special reason for excavation it should be left as it is.

I suggest repair only to the eastern bastion outside the castle. It

* This wall is no longer standing.

should be rebuilt with the old stones which are probably on the slope below the bastion.

I also suggest for the purpose of repair two good masons and labourers as required.

COST

Repairs to walling externally and pointing	£675
Interior repair and strengthening of modern walls and generally work inside	£200
Repair of corner towers and inner surface of upper walls	£200
Concrete roof	£230
Repair of east bastion	£125
	£1,430

The report is illustrated by six protographs taken at the time, (1928) which show :

1. The presence of a large earthen waste pipe under the old east door. This pipe has since been broken and was probably used as the waste pipe from the cottages.
2. That the small arc-shaped stone construction in the east wall near the north-east corner no longer holds the flagpole as it does in the photograph in Loyd's book (1925).
3. That the flagpole had been removed to the parade in front of the old door and was there standing on a concrete base and supported by a number of cables attached to various places on the parade.

SELECTED BIBLIOGRAPHY

ADMIRALTY RECORDS. Public Record Office, ADM 116/957–8–9, 116/982

ANSON, WALTER V. *The Life of Admiral Sir John Borlase Warren,* 1912; *The Life of Admiral Sir J. B. Warren,* 1914.

Antiquaries Journal, October 1923, vol 3, no 4

BARFIELD, J. A. *A Guide to North Devon,* c. 1843.

BARING-GOULD, S. *Devonshire Characters and Strange Events,* 1908

Bideford & North Devon Gazette

BOGGIS, REV E. *History of the Diocese of Exeter,* 1922

BOUNDY, WYNDHAM S. *Bushell and Harman of Lundy,* 1961

British Numismatic Journal, 1927–8, vol 19; 1929–30, vol 20

BRITTON and BRAYLEY. *Beauties of England and Wales,* vol 14, 1803

BROOKS, E. ST. JOHN. 'The Marisco Family of Lundy and Ireland' in *Journal of the Royal Society of Antiquaries of Ireland,* vol 61, 22–38 and 89–112, 1931

BURTON, S. H. *The North Devon Coast,* 1953

BUSHELL, THOMAS. A Brief Declaration . . . the Treaty Concerning the Surrender of the Garrison of Lundy, 1647; Humble Petition, 1660; Petitionary Remonstrance, 1663 (?); The Particular Services done by T. B., 1667

CAMDEN. *Britannia,* 1637 edition

CHANTER, J. R. *Lundy Island—A Monograph,* 1887

The Charters etc of Cleeve Abbey, 1865

Collectania Topographica et Genealogica, 1834–1843

The Complete Peerage, 1949, vol XI, appendix D, pp 107–8

Current Archaeology, no 8, May 1968

DASENT, SIR G. W. *Icelandic Sagas,* 1894, vol 3

DAVIDSON, E. H. 'Age of Lundy Island Granite' in *Geological Magazine,* February 1932

DAVIS, P. *A List of the Birds of Lundy,* Lundy Field Society, 1954

DEACON, R. *Madoc and the Discovery of America,* 1967

Devon and Cornwall Notes and Queries

Devon and Exeter Gazette

The Devon Feet of Fines, vol 2, Devon and Cornwall Record Society

Dictionary of National Biography

DOLLAR, DR A. T. J. 'The Lundy Complex : Petrology and Tectonics' in *Quarterly Journal of the Geological Society*, September, 1941; 'Abbreviated Interim Report of Investigations . . . Neolithic Man on Lundy Island', MS in North Devon Athenaeum, 1932

DOLLAR, DR A. T. J. 'Age Problems of Lundy Island Granite' in *Geological Magazine*, June 1932

English Historical Review, vols 10 and 62

FARR, GRAHAM E. *West Country Passenger Steamers*, 1956; *Wreck and Rescue in the Bristol Channel*, 1966

FIENNES, CELIA. *Through England on a Side-Saddle*, 1965

FULLER, B. and LESLIE-MELVILLE R. *Pirate Harbours and their Secrets*, 1935

GADE, F. W. *A Brief Postal History of Lundy*, 1957

GARDINER, W. F. *Barnstaple 1837–1897*

Gentleman's Magazine, 1754, 1755 and 1889

GOOSE, P. H. *Land and Sea*, 1864

GOUGH, J. W. *The Superlative Prodigal*, 1932, (A biography of Thomas Bushell)

GRANVILLE, Roger. *History of the Granville Family*, 1895

GROSE, F. *The Antiquities of England and Wales*, 1776, vol 4, pp 191–6

GURNEY, J. H. *The Gannet*, 1913

HARPER, C. G. *North Devon Coast*, 1908

Hartland Chronicle, 1906 'Benson, M. P. and Smuggler'

Home Friend, no 47, part 15, 1853

Journal of the Royal Institution of Cornwall, no 69, 1922

LANGHAM, A. and M. *Lundy, Bristol Channel*, 1960

LAWRENCE, JOHN. *A History of Capital Punishment*

LOYD, L. R. W. *Lundy, Its History and Natural History*, 1925

LUNDY FIELD SOCIETY. *Annual Reports*, 1947 to date

LYSONS, D. and S. *Magna Britannia*, 1822

MITCHELL, G. F. 'Glacial Gravel on Lundy Island', *Trans. Royal Geological Society*, vol 20, 1965–6

MONTMORENCY, H. G. DE. *A Memorandum explaining the claim of the Morres family to bear the name of Montmorency*, 1938

MONTMORENCY-MORRES, COL H. *Les Montmorency de France et Les Montmorency d'Irland*, 1828

North Devon Journal Herald

North Devon Magazine, containing the Cave and Lundy Review, vols 1 and 2, 1824 (Containing the 'Journal of 1787')

Notes and Queries 3rd Series, vol 1; 4th Series, vol 9; 7th Series, vol 11; 8th Series, vol 10; 8th Series, vol 11; 10th Series, vol 3. New Series, 21.6.1930.

Once a Week, 25.1.1862.

Orkneyinga Saga, Trans. A. B. Taylor, 1938

ORMONDE. *Calender of Ormonde Deeds,* 1932–43, Ed. E. Curtis

OSBORNE, DOROTHY. *Letters to Sir William Temple 1652–54,* 1928

PAGE, J. L. W. *The Coasts of Devon and Lundy Island,* 1895

PALMER, MERVYN G. *Ilfracombe Fauna and Flora,* 1946

PARIS, MATTHEW. *Chronica Majora,* Ed. Luard.

PARIS, MATTHEW. *Drawings of Matthew Paris,* Ed. M. R. James, publ. by Walpole Society, 1926

PERRY, RICHARD. *Lundy, Isle of Puffins,* 1940

POWICKE, F. M. 'The Murder of Henry Clement and the Pirates of Lundy Island, in *History,* vol 25, no 100, March 1941

RECEIVERS' ACCOUNTS. Somerset Exch. Land Revenue Series I (L.R.6), 15/6 38 Hen 8–3 Eliz.

Register of the Bishops of Exeter

RHYS, E. *The South Wales Coast,* 1911

RICHMOND, L. A. *Roman Britain,* 1955

RISDON, TRISTRAM. *Survey of the County of Devon,* 1714; *The Chorographical Description of Devon,* 1723

ROGERS, INKERMAN. *Lundy Island,* 1938

ROLLS : All references have been taken from the printed editions in the British Museum :

   Pipe Rolls
   Hundred Rolls
   Close Rolls
   Calendar Rolls
   Charter Rolls
   Curia Regis Rolls
   Fine Rolls
   Patent Rolls
   Liberate Rolls
   Chronicles of England
   Letters and Papers of Henry VIII
   Calendar of State Papers
   Book of Fees
   Calendar of Inquisitions Post-Mortem

ROWCROFT, W. *Local Post Issues*

ROYAL COMMISSIONERS ON HARBOURS OF REFUGE, *Report* 1859

ST CLAIRE, A. *Short History and Illustrated Guide to Lundy Island,* 1910

Saxon Chronicle

STANNARD, J. D. *Lundy Island and the Lundy Locals*, 1938

STEINMAN, G. S. *Some Account of the Island of Lundy*, Col Top. et Gen, 1837

STEVENSON, REV J. *The Church Historians of England Containing the Chronicle of Melrose*, vol 4, 1856

The Times: 19 May 1956; 20 August 1885; 14 January 1931; 10 September 1917; 14 February 1951; 7 December 1954; 6 September 1957; 12 May 1958; 7 December 1959.

THOMAS, STANLEY. *The Nightingale Scandal*, 1959 (Concerning Benson)

Transactions of the Devonshire Association, 1871, 1886, 1915

Travels of Sir William Brereton publ Chetham Society, vol 1, 1844

VICTORIA COUNTY HISTORIES : *Devon; Cornwall; Somerset*

WATERS, B. *The Bristol Channel*, 1955

WATT-SMYRKE, J. *Lundy*, 1936

Weekly Mercury

Western Morning News

WILLIAMS, NEVILLE. *Captains Outrageous*, 1961

WRIGHT, DR F. R. E. 'On the Origins of Lundy Flora, with Some Additions' in the *Journal of Botany*, April 1935

ACKNOWLEDGMENTS

We are very grateful to Mr K. S. Gardner for his kind contribution of a chapter and an appendix on the archaeology of Lundy. It has been the subject of his researches over many years and he has made a great contribution both to our knowledge of the island's past and to the understanding of what remains there today.

Our grateful acknowledgments are also made to the following : Miss E. Heaven, who lent us family papers and some notes about Lundy which had been made by her mother, the late Mrs M. C. H. Heaven; Canon J. S. Wright, who helped us with Latin translations and who also read through the original manuscript; Mr F. W. Gade, agent on the island since 1926, who provided us with a great deal of information and help; the late Mr A. E. Blackwell who, as curator of the North Devon Athenaeum and an unpublished author on the subject of Lundy himself, most generously gave us research material and other help; Mr M. R. Bouquet, for his help on maritime matters; Dr W. S. Bristow and Dr A. T. J. Dollar, who allowed us to use the results of their archaeological work and to Professor L. A. Harvey, who checked the lists of flora and fauna.

We would also like to thank many Lundy friends for their encouragement, and for their help in drawing our attention to various items concerning the island.

MYRTLE LANGHAM
ANTHONY LANGHAM

INDEX

211

INDEX

INDEX

INDEX